FROM CHILD TO CAREGIVER

LINDA H. WILLIAMS

FROM CHILD TO CAREGIVER

How to Navigate Your New Norm

Linda H. Williams

Pearly Gates Publishing, LLC, Harlem, GA (USA)

From Child to Caregiver:
How to Navigate Your New Norm

Copyright © 2022
Linda H. Williams

All Rights Reserved.
In accordance with the U.S. Copyright Act of 1976, the scanning, uploading, and electronic sharing of any part of this book without the author's or publisher's permission is unlawful piracy and theft of the author's intellectual property. If you would like to use material from this book (other than brief quotations for literary reviews), we ask you to please cite your reference.
Thank you for your support of the author's rights.

Disclaimer: The information presented is the author's opinion and does not constitute any health or medical advice. The content of this book is for informational purposes only and is not intended to diagnose, treat, cure, or prevent any condition or disease. Please seek advice from your healthcare provider for your personal health concerns prior to taking healthcare advice from this publication.

Cover Design Concept By:
Tia Jones

Print ISBN 13: 978-1-948853-54-5
Digital ISBN 13: 978-1-954188-11-2
Library of Congress Control Number: 2023930517

Pearly Gates Publishing, LLC
Angela Edwards, CEO
P.O. Box 639
Harlem, GA 30814
BestSeller@PearlyGatesPublishing.com

Acknowledgments

First and foremost, I thank God for giving me the gift of writing and the spirit to help others.

To my Mom and Dad, Rev. & Mrs. John T. Hilliard: Thank you for instilling in all of us the spirit of helping each other. We were taught that we don't fight against each other; we fight for each other.

To my brothers and sisters, Darryl T. Hilliard, Vicki L. Poole, and Faney L. Foster: Thank you for just being you and working together to care for our Daddy. A special thanks to Faney and William for opening your home to provide a safe haven for Daddy.

To Pastor Jason Keith and the members of the Humboldt Parkway Baptist Church in Buffalo, NY: Thank you for your support. A special thank you goes to Michelle Broadnax, who started looking after Mom and Dad a long time ago, even before they realized it. Thank you all for your love. Thank you to Chandra Gaddis (CNA), who loves and helps us take care of Daddy as if she were one of his daughters. Our lives are so blessed and enriched by their love.

Lastly, I want to thank and acknowledge all of those who have been given the task of caring for an elderly loved one and are trying to do the best they can.

Introduction

After 69 years of marriage and taking care of Daddy, Mama went home to be with the Lord. I recall Daddy saying, "I don't need nobody taking care of me. I'm alright!"—and he did well until COVID-19 hit in March 2020. He went from being a young, healthy 93-year-old to the man my sisters found passed out in the middle of the floor one day. Somebody needed to take care of Daddy, but we didn't know what to do!

A recent study revealed an increase in the number of family caregivers in the United States of 9.5 million from 2015 to 2020. Family caregivers now encompass more than one in five Americans. Becoming your parents' caretaker can be challenging to adapt to as it highlights a change in your parents' lives as well as a new chapter in your relationship. Furthermore, being a caregiver is a large responsibility that requires a lot of work, sacrifice, and time. Learning when to step in and setting expectations for what your parents need, along with what you can handle, is crucial. Whoever bears the burden of caring for the aged is often stressed by the developmental tasks of middle age. They are frequently unprepared for the role of caregiver—the moment they become a parent to their parents.

Most older adults don't need much help from others. In fact, many are quite busy assisting others and otherwise contributing to their families, communities, and/or workplaces. Still, many older people eventually **do** need some help from others, especially if they live into their 80s, 90s, or beyond. After all, only a minority of people transition from being fully independent to deceased, with no intervening period of needing assistance.

When an older person does start to need help, it tends to be close family members—assuming the person has a family—that step in (i.e., spouses, adult children, siblings, etc.). In fact, family members are by far the number one source of "long-term care support and services" for older adults. Sometimes, providing eldercare support can be fairly straightforward: a little help with transportation, arranging for some assistance with shopping, or household chores.

One of the most significant decisions a family may have to make is determining how to provide care for elderly parents or relatives when those elders are no longer able to live independently. Families resolve that complex and emotionally charged issue in a variety of ways. Some find ways to provide elderly people with sufficient assistance so that they can safely remain in their own homes. Others move their elders into their homes to personally provide care. Still others find that placing their elders in a care facility is the best solution for all involved.

Finding appropriate and affordable elder care and assistance is challenging. Determining exactly what type of care will best fit elders' needs is a time-consuming process that often requires consultations with medical and eldercare professionals. Locating affordable, appropriate, and reliable care options is also time-consuming. Different types of care are available in different places, while costs and quality vary widely. Identifying and locating appropriate and affordable local eldercare resources can become a full-time job that is stressful for all participants. Even employers and coworkers can be affected when the strain of eldercare planning makes caregivers less effective at their workplace.

Caring for someone you love who has taken care of you is a daunting task. Between my brother, two sisters, and myself, we kind of fell into a rhythm of taking care of and providing for our Dad. My sister, Faney, provides a home and takes care of all of Daddy's finances. My other sister, Vicki, takes care of all of Daddy's medical needs. My brother, Darryl, provides home healthcare for Daddy, and I take care of all the business needs in caring for him. That arrangement is the best of all possible scenarios, but what I have learned is that is not the norm. More often than not, there is only one sibling handling all of their elderly parents' needs.

This book draws on the experiences my siblings and I have had while caring for our Daddy for the past several years. It is my hope this resource will provide guidance and help others deal with everything that comes with going "From Child to Caregiver."

Table of Contents

Acknowledgments vi

Introduction vii

Chapter 1 1

   Health & Medical 1

Chapter 2 13

   Financials 13

Chapter 3 43

   Handling Business 43

Chapter 4 71

   Emotional Daily Living 71

Chapter 5 92

   Caregiver 92

Resources 108

In Conclusion.. 128

About the Author 130

Chapter 1
Health & Medical

*"To care for those who once cared for us
is one of the highest honors."*
~ Tia Walker ~

Today, we can expect to live longer than ever before. Once you make it to 65, the data suggests that you can live another 19.3 years on average, according to the Centers for Disease Control and Prevention (CDC). For many of us, senior living includes carefully managing chronic conditions in order to stay healthy.

Medical concerns are fairly common later in life. Many of us have chronic conditions that require medications, monitoring, and other forms of ongoing management. Older adults may also develop new symptoms or health concerns that may require their family's assistance in coping. Most people will also need help when recovering from an illness. Serious illnesses or chronic conditions can cause older adults to lose the ability to make their health decisions or oversee their own medical care. As a result, family members must often make decisions due to a health emergency or mental decline.

An older person's medical situation often affects their ability to manage activities of daily living (ADL), instrumental activities of daily living (IADL), and their caregiving needs. The intensity of the medical situation also affects how much time their family spends dealing with those health issues, which often affect everyone's quality of life.

1. **Chronic Health Conditions:** According to the National Council on Aging, about 92 percent of seniors have at least one chronic disease, and 77 percent have at least two. Heart disease, stroke, cancer, and diabetes are among the most common and costly chronic health conditions, causing two-thirds of deaths each year.

    a. **Heart Disease:** According to the CDC, heart disease remains the leading killer of adults over age 65, accounting for approximately 659,000 deaths per year. As a chronic condition, heart disease affects 37 percent of men and 26 percent of women 65 and older, according to the Federal Interagency Forum on Aging-Related Statistics. As your loved one ages, they're increasingly living with risk factors that increase the chances of having a stroke or developing heart disease. High blood pressure, high cholesterol, obesity, smoking, poor eating habits, and inactivity are a few of the leading causes. It is imperative that you, as the caregiver, are aware of the factors related to chronic heart disease. Whether your loved one has had heart issues or not, as we age, the likelihood will increase. Addressing this senior health risk not only helps identify risk factors but can also improve senior health across the board. Keeping your loved one's heart healthy will help prolong their life and increase the chances of quality life. "Exercise, eat well, and get a good night's rest."

b. **Cancer:** Cancer is the second leading cause of death among people over age 65, with approximately 440,000 deaths yearly, according to the CDC. The CDC also reports that 28 percent of men and 21 percent of women over age 65 are living with cancer. Even if our nutritional status, physical activity, and other environmental factors are at their best, it is not possible to keep away from cancer. Along with our physiological aging process, processes that control the proliferation of cells will weaken, our repair mechanisms slow down, and cellular destructive changes can often accumulate. Given that, even if our loved ones are healthy individuals and have not shown any signs of the disease, cancer screening tests should be performed for early diagnosis to increase the chances of a cure. If caught early, many types of cancer are treatable. Early detection of the disease yields better outcomes for treatment and care, even as a senior adult.

c. **Following are some suggestions on how you can help your loved one improve their quality of life as a senior.**
   - Avoid tobacco use. Using any type of tobacco puts them on a collision course with cancer.
   - Provide a healthy diet.
   - Maintain a healthy weight and be physically active.
   - Protect them from the sun.
   - Get them vaccinated.
   - Avoid risky behaviors.
   - Get regular medical care.
d. **Respiratory Diseases:** Chronic lower-respiratory diseases, such as chronic pulmonary disease (COPD), bronchitis, emphysema, and asthma, are the third most common cause of death among people 65 and older. Those chronic health conditions cause approximately 300,000 deaths annually in older adults, according to the CDC. Among people 65 and older, about 10 percent of men and 13 percent of women are living with asthma, and 10 percent of men and 11 percent of women are living with chronic bronchitis or emphysema, according to the Federal Interagency Forum on Aging-Related Statistics. Although having a chronic respiratory

disease increases senior health risks—making the elderly more vulnerable to pneumonia and other infections—getting lung function tests, taking the correct medications, and using oxygen as instructed will go a long way in preserving senior health and the quality of life of your loved one. The leading causes of respiratory ailments are:

- Infections.
- Smoking tobacco.
- Breathing in secondhand tobacco smoke.
- Asbestos and other forms of air pollution.

Note: *Just because we age does not mean we will automatically have diminished respiratory health. Even as we care for our loved ones, there are ways to greatly decrease and/or improve their health and ours as we age.*

Recommendations

- **Don't smoke—or stop smoking ASAP.** The CDC has found that cigarettes are the leading cause of preventable deaths in the United States. It's never too late to stop smoking. It won't reverse the damage that has been done, but it can greatly slow the negative effects. It has also been established that secondhand smoke can be just as detrimental, if not more so.

- **Get health screenings regularly.** As you care for your elderly loved ones, it is imperative that you stay on top of annual physicals. You might also ask to have a breathing test (known as a Pulmonary Function Test) prescribed, especially if they are or have been a smoker. The test is noninvasive and will demonstrate how well the lungs are working. The test measures lung volume, capacity, rate of flow, and gas exchange. The results can assist the healthcare provider with diagnosing and deciding the treatment of certain lung disorders.
- **Develop a regular exercise routine.** You must keep your elders moving. Exercise not only helps reduce or minimize muscle atrophy in the chest, but it also keeps other muscles and joints healthy. In other words, exercise allows the lungs to open more fully. Deep breathing exercises help to ensure the air cells of the lungs remain strong and healthy, which can help ward off pneumonia.
- **Be aware of pollutants that can cause illnesses.** Secondhand cigarette smoke, dust, artificial air fresheners, and candles can irritate the lungs. Try to eliminate pet dander and use natural cleaning products, ensuring there is adequate ventilation in bathrooms and kitchens when cleaning.
- **Practice Self-Care.** Drink plenty of liquids. To keep the immune system strong, seniors need to stay hydrated

every day. Incorporating plenty of fruits and vegetables into their diet can help keep the immune system strong, too.

- e. **Cognitive and Mental Health: Cognitive health** is focused on a person's ability to think, learn, and remember. The most common cognitive health issue facing the elderly is dementia—the loss of those cognitive functions. The most common form of dementia is Alzheimer's Disease, with as many as five million people over the age of 65 suffering from the disease in the United States. According to the National Institute on Aging, other chronic health conditions and diseases increase the risk of developing dementia, such as substance abuse, diabetes, hypertension, depression, HIV, and smoking. While there are no cures for dementia, physicians can prescribe a treatment plan and medications to manage the disease. Experts acknowledge that cognitive impairment has a significant impact on senior health across the spectrum—from issues of safety and self-care to the cost burden of care, either in the home or a residential facility.

    Although it can get increasingly more difficult to communicate with your loved one suffering from

dementia, here are some suggestions that might help:
- Limit potential distractions.
- Speak naturally and use gestures.
- Use your name and others' names.
- Talk about one thing at a time.
- Use nonverbal cues.
- Avoid overwhelming questions.
- Be creative.
- Be patient and avoid jumping in.
- It's never a good idea to argue with a person who has dementia. Even if they don't understand their errors, correcting them may embarrass or be unpleasant for them.

Mental health: A common mental disorder among seniors is depression, occurring in seven percent of the elderly population. Unfortunately, this mental disorder is often underdiagnosed and undertreated. Depression is a threat to mental health that can lower immunity and compromise a person's ability to fight infections. It can affect every aspect of your loved one's life by impacting their energy, appetite, sleep, interest in work, hobbies, and relationships. Ultimately, it will also impact the quality of your life as a caregiver. If your loved one is suffering from depression, here are some suggestions that might help:

    i.   Treat sleeping problems.
    ii.   Promote a sense of purpose.
    iii.   Encourage social interaction.
    iv.   Keep them physically active.
    v.   Make sure they eat healthily.
    vi.   Entrust them with a chore.
    vii.   Show them they are loved.
    viii.   Seek professional help.

f. **Physical Injury:** Every 15 seconds, an older adult is admitted to the emergency room for a fall, making it the leading cause of injury among the elderly. One-third of people who go to the hospital for a fall may find themselves there again within one year, according to a study recently published in the American Journal of Emergency Medicine. Because aging causes bones to shrink and muscle to lose strength and flexibility, seniors are more susceptible to losing their balance, bruising, and fracturing a bone. While most falls occur in the home, they are not inevitable. You can decrease the likelihood of your loved one falling by:

- Cleaning up clutter.
- Repairing or removing tripping hazards (i.e., area rugs and slippery bathroom floors).

- Installing grab bars and handrails.
- Avoiding wearing loose clothing.
- Ensuring areas are well-lit.
- Ensuring they wear nonslip footwear.
- Living on one level of the home.

g. **Oral Hygiene:** Often overlooked, oral health is one of the most important issues for the elderly. The CDC's Division of Oral Health found that about 25 percent of adults over the age of 65 no longer have their natural teeth. Problems such as cavities and tooth decay can lead to difficulties maintaining a healthy diet, low self-esteem, and other health conditions. Oral health is a significant factor affecting older adults' quality of life, overall health, and well-being. Tooth loss, tooth decay (dental caries), gum disease (periodontitis), dry mouth (xerostomia), and oral cancers are commonly experienced by older people. These conditions can be prevented or managed by:

- Brushing at least twice a day with fluoride-containing toothpaste.
- Flossing at least once a day.
- Rinsing with an antiseptic mouthwash once or twice a day.

- Visiting the dentist regularly for cleanings and oral exams. Dental care can be difficult for seniors to access due to loss of dental insurance after retirement or economical disadvantages.

h. **Bladder Control and Constipation:** Incontinence and constipation are both common with aging and can impact older adults' quality of life. In addition to age-related changes, they may be a side-effect of previous issues, such as not eating a well-balanced diet and suffering from chronic health conditions. A recent study by the Mayo Clinic suggests that having your loved one maintain a healthy weight, eat a healthy diet, and exercise regularly can help to avoid these elderly health issues. These conditions can become quite burdensome for the caregiver, so the following self-help tips and lifestyle changes can relieve some of your elderly parents' symptoms:

- Do daily pelvic floor exercises.
- Stop smoking.
- Do the correct exercises.
- Avoid lifting.
- Lose excess weight.
- Treat constipation promptly.
- Reduce caffeine consumption.

- Reduce alcohol consumption.

There are often effective medical treatments, and you should not be embarrassed to discuss them with your loved one's physicians.

Aging can bring about unique health issues. With seniors accounting for 12 percent of the world's population—and estimates that it will increase to 22 percent by 2050—it's important to understand the health and medical challenges faced by people as they age and how it impacts your life as a caregiver.

Chapter 2
Financials

"Beware of little expenses. A small leak will sink a great ship."
~ Benjamin Franklin ~

Part 1 – Handling your elderly parents' financial business

Your parents raised you, loved you, and provided financial security as you grew up. Now that you're grown and have a family of your own, the roles are reversed: You're a caregiver to your aging parents. Perhaps they need help managing day-to-day affairs, such as finances and/or household maintenance. Many people worry about the ability of their aging parents and other loved ones to handle money and financial affairs. Many older adults need assistance because of situations including:

- mental impairments.
- visual impairments.
- physical impairments (i.e., arthritis) that limit the ability to write checks or sign documents.
- loss of a spouse who handled all the finances.
- for immigrants, lack of English skills or familiarity with banking and tax procedures.
- increased vulnerability to scammers.

When your elderly loved ones cannot handle daily finances or become more susceptible to financial abuse, the consequences can be severe. If they forget to pay bills, they could lose their home to foreclosure, face eviction from an apartment, risk utility shut-off, or damage their credit. Those who fall victim to scams might get cheated out of large amounts of money or lose their home. Sometimes, your older loved one may need a guardian or conservator to take control of their finances and medical decisions. Guardians and conservators can be family members or other adults, but they must have the legal authority to make those decisions on the elderly person's behalf—either through legal documentation (Power of Attorney) or appointed by the court. Where do you start?

1. **Assess the situation.** The first step in assisting your elderly parent or relative with money management is determining if they need help. If they do, how much help is needed? Start by talking with your elderly relative. In some situations, the financial needs of the elderly are apparent. Some seniors may admit they need help and will welcome your assistance. Others will insist they can handle their affairs and resist intervention. If your relative falls into the latter category, but you see signs that assistance is necessary, do some investigating.
    a. Look around your older relative's home. Do you see a lot of unopened mail, bills scattered around, or piles of papers? Can the elder show you an

organized filing system or describe how they manage their money?

b. Talk to your older relative's doctors, friends, and other family members. What do they say about your relative's mental capacity? Have they seen signs of confusion or increasing forgetfulness?

c. Go through your elderly relative's checkbook, credit card statements, and bank statements. Look for anything unusual, including double entries for the same item, questionable transactions, transfers involving large amounts of money, several small transfers, a change in banking habits, or payments to unknown entities.

d. Ask the elder to explain large payments to entities or people unknown to you. (Often, the elder's explanation will give you an idea of their ability to handle their own financial affairs.)

e. If the elder pays the mortgage, rent, or other monthly expenses by check, do you see consistent entries for those items in the checkbook?

f. Has the elder received account alerts or letters from collection agencies?

g. Does the elder fail to open and pay bills, cash checks, record checks, or list deposits?

h. Are checkbooks, bank statements, or other financial documents missing or hard to find?

i. Does the elder seem confused or forgetful?
   j. Has the elder spent large amounts of money on things such as lotteries, contests, or items from the Home Shopping Network?
   k. Has the elder made unusually large donations to charitable organizations or other groups?
   l. Does the elder know what bank accounts and investments they have?
   m. Has the elder been the victim of a financial scam, such as telemarketing fraud, investment fraud, identity theft, or predatory lending?
2. **Broaching the subject.** It is important to broach the subject of financial assistance with sensitivity. Your elderly loved one may be embarrassed by their inability to handle their financial affairs. They may also be afraid that by relinquishing their control of money, they are losing a large measure of independence. Some believe that children or relatives want to steal their money. Often, the best time to discuss finances for the elderly is before they need help.
   a. Discuss what will happen if and when they need help managing their finances. Agree on some "trigger" events that might indicate they need help (i.e., receiving account alerts), and devise a plan to work together if that time comes.

b. Explain your concerns about certain aspects of money management and point out possible consequences if things remain as they are (i.e., foreclosure, closed accounts, or damaged credit).
c. Involve your elderly relative in the decision-making process as much as possible.
d. Keep the focus on what they can do. Make suggestions only for those tasks that you feel they need help with.
e. Most importantly, listen to what they have to say about the issue.

Those conversations can be difficult and emotional for all parties involved. Before you dive in, consider getting guidance from a financial expert on elder issues.

3. **Locate important documents.** Getting your older loved ones to accept help with their financials can take major effort and patience. It is imperative that you have a handle on it, and a big step in accomplishing the task is having access to their important documents. In addition to managing your own finances, the thought of managing someone else's can seem daunting. So, where do you start?

   a. Gather your parents' personal information, making a record of where it's all kept.
   b. Make a comprehensive list of all financial and investment accounts, including household

utilities, credit card accounts, and mortgage or rental information.

c. Collect all statements and documents for the financial and investment accounts.

d. Create a payment schedule for all bills, such as mortgage, telephone, property tax, and homeowner's insurance.

e. Start submitting timely payments according to the payment schedule.

f. Take inventory of your parents' safe deposit box (if they have one) and bring along a witness.

g. Determine if their legal documents require updating.

4. **Decide whether to seek professional assistance**. Reaching out to professionals for their help to ensure your parents have all their financial ducks in a row is a good idea. They can help you to better understand their financial status, ensure you're doing everything correctly, and thus, relieve a lot of your stress.

   a. **Estate Planning Attorney.** An estate planning attorney's area of concentration focuses on legal documents concerning your loved one's property after their death, often in a way that minimizes tax liability. They can also prepare legal documents that give you the authority to make financial and medical decisions on your parents' behalf.

Documents such as a durable Power of Attorney and a Living Will are quite useful—and sometimes necessary—to facilitate proper and responsible management of your loved one's affairs. This attorney can also assist with setting up a care plan for your loved one's long-term care.

    b. **Financial Planner or Advisor.** If your parents are blessed with a certain wealth, seeking the help of a financial planner or advisor to help manage their assets can take a heavy load off your mind. Your parents may have a variety of assets or complex investments that require knowledge from a professional financial perspective.

5. **Gain access to financial accounts.** Getting access to your older loved one's bank accounts requires advance planning and likely some specific paperwork. What would happen if you had to suddenly take over management of your parent's finances? If your mother or father were to fall ill or become incapacitated, someone must continue paying their bills and managing their money. That scenario happens in many families. Are you prepared?

    a. Banks and other financial institutions have strict rules about who can access accounts. Often, they require their own documents to be completed, even if you already have a Power of Attorney.

    b. To write checks or withdraw money from your older adult's accounts, you could become authorized to conduct transactions.

    c. To get access to a safe deposit box, your older loved one can authorize a "deputy" or "agent."

    d. In addition to knowing where they keep their money, you need specifics on all their accounts. What bank(s) do they use? Who is their mortgage company? Do they use an investment company or work with a broker?

6. **Keep the family informed.** Your older adult should stay involved in their financial decisions as long as they can. If that's not possible and you need to take full responsibility, it's wise to share information with other family members or involve them in the process. Doing so helps avoid conflicts later, such as one person accusing another of inappropriately spending the older adult's money "behind the family's back."

    a. Holding family meetings to discuss finances is a good way to keep everyone up to date on spending and income. Although emotions are sure to run high, it is possible to conduct a productive meeting by following a few guidelines.

        i. Set an agenda for the meeting and adhere to it.

ii. Focus on the "here and now." Try not to bring up past or unrelated issues.
iii. Share your feelings with siblings instead of being accusatory.
iv. Listen to and respect the opinions of all participants.
v. It's also smart to maintain a record of significant discussions, decisions, and actions in case there are disputes in the future.

Part 2: The cost of care

Older adults and their families strive each day to pay for healthcare and medicine, keep food on the table, maintain a roof over their heads, and have enough cash on hand to pay the utilities, get to where they need to go, and meet other basic needs. While we are often concentrating on ensuring our loved one's affairs are in order, we fail to realize the task of considering the day-to-day needs.

1. **Healthcare.** This is the category that hits many senior adults' retirement expenses the hardest because of the obvious surge in medical needs as they age. An article from CNN Money estimates that the average 65-year-old man will spend $189,687 on healthcare in retirement, while an average 65-year-old woman will spend $214,565. Because medical situations and attendant

costs are unpredictable, they are one of the key reasons you must investigate all avenues of aiding your aging loved ones.

    a. **Medicare.** Medicare is a federal health insurance program for people 65 years or older, certain people with disabilities, and people with end-stage renal disease (ESRD). If your loved one is over 65, they should already be enrolled in Medicare. When they first enroll, they'll have Original Medicare, unless they make another choice. There are different ways to get Medicare coverage, including a Medicare Advantage Plan (like an HMO or PPO). In some types of plans that don't offer prescription drug coverage, you may be able to join a Medicare Prescription Drug Plan.

        i. Get detailed information about the Medicare health and prescription drug plans in your area, including what they cost and what services they provide.

        ii. Find doctors and other healthcare providers and supplies that participate in Medicare.

        iii. See what Medicare covers, including preventative services, dental, and vision.

        iv. Get Medicare appeals information and forms.

v. Get information about the quality of care provided by plans, nursing homes, hospitals, home health agencies, and dialysis facilities.

b. **Medicare prescription drug coverage.** Since January 1, 2006, everyone with Medicare—regardless of income, health status, or prescription drug usage—has had access to prescription drug coverage. For more information about this program, visit the following website: www.medicare.gov/part-d/index.html. Medicare offers prescription drug coverage to everyone with Medicare. If your loved one decided not to join a Medicare Prescription Drug Plan (Part D) when they were first eligible and they don't have other creditable prescription drug coverage or get Extra Help, they'll likely pay a late-enrollment penalty. To get Medicare drug coverage, they must join a plan run by an insurance company or other private company approved by Medicare. Each plan can vary in cost and drugs covered. There are two ways to get drug coverage:

  i. A Medicare Prescription Drug Plan (Part D).
  ii. A Medicare Advantage Plan (Part C), like an HMO or PPO, or other Medicare health

plan that offers Medicare prescription drug coverage.

c. **Medicaid.** Medicaid is a joint federal and state program that provides free or low-cost health coverage to millions of Americans, including some low-income people, families and children, pregnant women, the elderly, and people with disabilities. The federal government provides a portion of the funding for Medicaid and sets guidelines for the program. Medicaid programs vary from state to state. They may also have different names, like "Medical Assistance" or "Medi-Cal." No matter your state, your loved one may qualify for Medicaid based on income, household size, disability, family status, and other factors. If your state has expanded Medicaid coverage, your loved one can qualify based on their income alone. Visit the website for your state to determine eligibility requirements.

d. **The Health Insurance Marketplace.** The Health Insurance Marketplace was created by the Affordable Care Act and helps you find health coverage that fits your needs and budget. Every health plan in the Marketplace offers the same set of essential health benefits, including doctor visits, preventive care, hospitalization, and more.

You can compare plans based on price, benefits, quality, and other features important to you before making a choice. People in most states use healthcare.gov to apply for and enroll in health coverage. With one application, you will see if your loved one qualifies for free or low-cost coverage through Medicaid or CHIP, or for savings on a Marketplace plan. Most people who apply will qualify for some kind of savings. For more information, visit healthcare.gov or call the Marketplace Call Center at 1-800-318-2596, 24 hours a day, 7 days a week. TTY users should call 1-855-889-4325. If your state runs its own Marketplace, you won't use healthcare.gov; you'll use your state's website to enroll in individual/family coverage, small business health coverage, or both.

2. **Food and Nutrition.** Of course, people over 65 continue to incur the same basic expenses as every other age group, and food is no exception. Seniors can save by using coupons and store discounts, but groceries and dining out still make up one of the major budget categories for older Americans. For the cost-conscious senior, eating at home is, by far, the more economical option, although travel and other obligations can make the convenience of restaurants much more tempting. An

example presented in a Motley Fool article speculated that if the average cost for a meal at a restaurant costs $50.00, the same food prepared at home would cost $12.50.

Having access to nutritious food directly affects a person's health and well-being. That is no less true for older adults. Seniors who are food insecure are over 50 percent more likely to report a heart attack and develop asthma, and 40 percent are more likely to experience congestive heart failure. Programs like the Supplemental Nutrition Assistance Program (SNAP) and Meals on Wheels are direct ways to combat the risk of hunger among older adults while helping them be able to pay for other necessities like medicine and housing. Research shows that, in addition to the other benefits of food security, when low-income seniors have access to programs like SNAP, they are less likely to experience hospitalization or be admitted into a nursing facility.

a. **SNAP** is a federal program that helps low-income households, including millions of older adults, pay for food. More than 1 in 10 SNAP recipients—nearly 5 million people—are age 60 or older, while 80 percent of older adults who depend on SNAP live alone. SNAP benefits are also critical for low-income older adult households, which, for the most part, live below the poverty line. Over 85 percent of SNAP households with elderly individuals receive income from Social Security or Supplemental Security Income (SSI).

   b. **Meals on Wheels** provides older adults with meals delivered to their homes or served in group settings, such as senior centers. Funds from the Older Americans Act cover about a third of the total cost of providing meals through Meals on Wheels, while state and local funds and private donations cover the rest.

3. **Personal Care.** Everyday tasks can become more difficult as we age. For many seniors, good personal hygiene can be especially challenging due to a lack of mobility and sometimes a sheer lack of energy. Depression, isolation, dementia, a fear of falling, or medication side effects can all cause seniors to lose interest in or completely neglect their personal hygiene and grooming. Health and hygiene go hand in hand. If you are concerned about your loved one's personal hygiene:

   a. **Identify the issues.** Get to the root of why your loved one has neglected their personal hygiene. Aging adults often develop poor hygiene because of mobility issues or because they are physically unable to perform their normal hygiene routines and are afraid to say something. Whatever the reason, it is important to identify the issues and discuss potential solutions to help them stay clean and healthy.

b. **Establish a routine.** Creating a daily hygiene routine can help your loved one get used to doing specific activities, such as showering and brushing their teeth and hair. Avoid making the routines seem like chores or something that must be rushed. Make it a part of their day by:
   i. Putting on the music they like.
   ii. Keeping the room, water, and towels warm.
   iii. Laying out their clothes so that they can slip into a comfortable outfit right away.

c. **Ensure the bathroom is safe.** The fear of falling or slipping can often be enough to prevent seniors from using a shower or bath altogether. Install the right equipment in the bathroom, such as handrails in the shower and near the toilet, raised toilet seats, and add a bench in the shower.

d. **Buy helpful hygiene aids.** There are many devices designed to solve elderly hygiene issues by making it easier for them to take care of their own personal grooming. Shower chairs, no-rinse bathing wipes, and long-handled shower brushes, razors, and toenail clippers can all make taking care of personal hygiene safer and easier.

e. **Consider hiring professional support.** A professional caregiver can provide personal hygiene services for your elderly loved one, who may actually prefer that option if he or she has been avoiding having to ask you or another family member for help. They may feel more comfortable having a non-family member perform those tasks. A good, dependable CNA can help with many activities concerning daily living, from bathing and oral hygiene to walking and mobility...and everything in between. There are many agencies that can provide those services to you and your loved one.

f. **Equipment and incontinence.** As activities related to daily living become more challenging for your aging loved ones, you might consider assistive devices to make life easier for them. Evaluate current living conditions to see if any of the following might provide much-needed help:

　i. Personal Alert System (a wearable electronic device designed to summon help in an emergency)

　ii. Toilet seat riser

iii. Grab bars for the bathroom near the toilet and shower
iv. Hand-held showerhead
v. Bathtub/shower transfer bench
vi. Stepless/walk-in bathtub or shower
vii. Adjustable bed
viii. Waterproof mattress/mattress pads
ix. Over-bed table
x. Disposable incontinence under pads, wipes, bedliners, etc.
xi. Bed railings
xii. Touchtone telephones with large buttons, a speaker, or hands-free capabilities, and/or text capability for those who are deaf or hard of hearing (TTY or TDD)
xiii. Automatic shut-off safety devices for kitchen appliances
xiv. Ramps for entryways with steps
xv. Stair lifts for multi-story homes
xvi. Sturdy railings along all stairways
xvii. Mobility aids for seniors who have difficulty getting around the house (i.e., cane, Hoyer lift, walker, wheelchair, motorized scooter)
xviii. Lift chairs for those who have difficulty getting in and out of a seated position

4. **Housing.** As our loved ones age, a decision must be made: Can they continue living on their own, live with one of their children, or be placed in an assisted living facility? That decision depends on a host of factors, including:
    a. **Independent Living.** From at-home care to senior apartments, people have many options for independent senior living.
        i. **Aging in place.** "Aging in place" is a term used to describe when an older person keeps living in their current home instead of moving to a retirement home. They often modify their current home to address any mobility issues, and they often work with home healthcare professionals to get assistance where needed. Although this option can have relatively low to medium costs, it only works best if your older adult is still relatively independent or can get the level of assistance they need.
        ii. **Independent living communities.** Independent living communities can go by a variety of names. They may be called retirement villages, active adult communities, or senior housing. Residents have their own private living space but also

get access to certain amenities that may be provided. They may be refurbished buildings designed exclusively for seniors who want to live in an active community setting, free from worries about daily chores like house maintenance, cooking, or housekeeping. The cost of this option can be from medium to high, depending on location and services.

iii. **Moving in with the kids.** Although certainly not for everyone, moving in with an adult child—or having them move in with the elder—can be a win-win. It can immediately slash living expenses in half. Plus, there's the possibility of fringe benefits for both parties. Busy parents may end up with built-in babysitting, while seniors (particularly those who are single) benefit from an active household that will stave off loneliness and the health risks linked to it. The key to making the arrangements work is to set clear guidelines from the start. Make sure everyone has the same expectations about communal living, personal space, and bill sharing.

b. **Assisted Living.** People suffering from certain illnesses and ailments need extra help with daily tasks. It can be hard to accept that your loved one needs help, but knowing all the options available can help you choose the right facility.

   i. **Assisted living facilities** are housing options that provide help with instrumental activities of daily living (IADLs), like cooking and bathing, but not necessarily a lot of medical assistance. Residents usually have a private or semi-private bedroom and bathroom, but they share all other areas. Offerings in assisted living facilities vary greatly. Typically, the facilities provide meals, housekeeping, laundry services, recreation and exercise activities, and transportation to doctors' appointments. Some might have a limited nursing staff for medical assistance. They could also have on-site beauty shops and entertainment venues.

   ii. **Nursing homes** are senior living facilities that offer a high level of medical care. Like assisted living facilities, nursing homes have numerous amenities and help with basic activities. However, they also provide medication management and 24-hour supervision, leading to a more clinical environment. If your loved one requires long-term medical assistance, you might consider this option. Nursing homes provide quality medical care to people with complex medical problems. The facilities are licensed and regulated by state agencies, so there's oversight to ensure they offer proper care.

iii. **Hospice care** is a type of care if your loved one has a terminal illness. People may receive hospice care in their homes or in nursing homes. Hospice focuses on providing services like pain management to make your loved one's life as comfortable as possible. This option is especially beneficial for anyone diagnosed with a life-limiting illness. Hospice is a good choice if you decide to transition your loved one to care that treats their symptoms instead of fighting their disease. The term "hospice" typically conjures up images of "end of life." However, it encompasses a wider range of services to make life more comfortable with whatever time your loved one has left.

As you take on responsibility for your loved one as they age, you'll have to think about housing options. There's a lot to consider, so make sure everyone involved has thought about their roles and priorities. Make sure you do your research, determine the needs of your loved one by talking to their doctors, and most importantly, consider the financial obligations of the cost of housing options.

5. **Transportation.** About 600,000 older adults stop driving each year, according to US Aging, the national association for Area Agencies on Aging. That can make it harder for your aging or ill loved ones to make doctors' appointments, shop for necessities, visit family, or attend social events. That, in turn, increases their isolation, which negatively affects their health and well-being. Transportation is often a major responsibility for caregivers. More than 40 percent of older and disabled adults rely on family, friends, and neighbors for rides. An estimated three-quarters of caregivers list providing or arranging transportation as one of their primary duties, according to a recent survey by the National Aging and Disability Transportation Center (NADTC), a program administered by US Aging and Easter Seals that promotes accessible transit.

Providing transportation is not always easy or convenient. "Some family caregivers just can't leave their job every time somebody needs a ride to the doctor, much less even to the grocery store," says Virginia Dize, a US Aging Program Director and Co-Director of the NADTC. Finding alternatives for times when you can't get your loved one where they need to go will require some research. A variety of options are available that can lessen the burden on you while helping your older and disabled loved ones keep appointments and stay socially connected.

    a. **Public Transportation.** Primarily bus and rail services, operated and financed by federal, state, and local governments, with fixed routes and set schedules, these systems usually offer discounted fares for older adults and people with disabilities. Vouchers may be available as well. Some transit agencies and local aging or disability organizations provide free training to help riders learn to travel safely. Buses, railcars, and stations usually have accessibility features, but public transit might not be a suitable alternative for people who have difficulty navigating stairs, waiting outside, or walking to and from stops.

    b. **Paratransit.** Public transit agencies are required by law to provide "complementary paratransit service" for people who are unable to use regular lines. Paratransit operates during the same hours as normal service and covers comparable routes. Riders must meet eligibility criteria set by the federal Americans with Disabilities Act (ADA). Vehicles are typically outfitted for accessibility. Trips should be scheduled at least one day in advance and are generally shared with other passengers who have booked similar times. Paratransit providers typically have a 30-minute pick-up window, from 15 minutes before to 15 minutes after the scheduled time, so riders need to be ready and waiting at least 15 minutes early.

c. **Ride-hailing.** Ride-hailing companies, such as Lyft and Uber, connect passengers with drivers who provide point-to-point transportation in their own vehicles. Booking and payment are typically done via mobile apps. In some cities, riders can request wheelchair assistance as part of their booking, and the companies have expanded accessibility efforts in recent years. The Uber Assist program trains drivers to accommodate passengers who have mobility issues and use wheelchairs, walkers, or scooters. Lyft has teamed up with United Way to provide free rides through the "211" phone service for people who have difficulty using public transit.

d. **Non-emergency medical transportation.** NEMT, as it is known, is a Medicaid benefit that covers travel to medical appointments. Private insurance, including some Medicare Advantage plans, may also cover non-emergency medical transit (check with your loved one's provider). Eligibility rules, types of destinations, and allowable modes of transport vary from state to state. Taxis, wheelchair vans, or vehicles dispatched by specialty brokers or community groups often provide the service, but a growing number of insurers and state Medicaid programs are covering the cost of Lyft and Uber rides.

Part 3: Paying for Care

Many older adults and caregivers worry about the cost of medical care. These expenses can use up a significant amount of monthly income, even for families who thought they had saved enough. The manner in which people pay for long-term care—whether delivered at home or in a hospital, assisted living facility, or nursing home—depends on their financial situation and the kinds of services they use. Often, they rely on a variety of payment sources, including personal funds, government programs, and private funding options.

- **Personal Funds (Out-of-Pocket Expenses).** At first, many older adults pay for care, in part, with their own money. They may use personal savings, a pension or other retirement fund, income from stocks and bonds, and/or proceeds from the sale of a home. Much home-based care is paid for using personal funds ("out-of-pocket"). Initially, family and friends often provide personal care and other services, such as transportation, for free. However, as a person's needs increase, paid services may be needed.
- **Government Programs.** Older adults may be eligible for some government healthcare benefits. Caregivers can help by learning more about possible sources of financial help and assisting older adults with applying for aid as appropriate. The Internet can be a helpful tool in the search. Several federal and state programs provide help with healthcare-related costs.
- **Center for Medicare and Medicaid Services (CMS).** This service agency offers several programs. Over time, the benefits and eligibility requirements of these programs can change, and some benefits differ from state to state. Check with CMS or the individual programs directly for the most recent information.
- **Medicare.** Medicare is a federal government health insurance program that pays some medical costs for people aged 65 and older, and for all people with late-

stage kidney failure. It also pays some medical costs for those who have gotten Social Security Disability Income for 24 months. It does not cover ongoing personal care at home, assisted living, or long-term care. Check your loved one's Medicare coverages (Parts A, B, D) for specific costs covered.

- **Medicaid.** Some people may qualify for Medicaid—a combined Federal and State program for low-income people and families. This program covers the costs of medical care and some forms of long-term care for people who have limited income and meet other eligibility requirements. Who is eligible and what services are covered vary from state to state. Visit the Medicaid.gov website or contact your state health department for eligibility requirements.
- **Program of All-Inclusive Care for the Elderly (PACE).** Some states have PACE—a Medicare program that provides care and services to people who otherwise would need nursing home care. PACE covers medical, social service, and long-term care costs for frail people. To find out more about PACE, visit the PACE website or Medicare's PACE page.
- **Department of Veterans Affairs.** The U.S. Department of Veterans Affairs (VA) may provide long-term care or at-home care for some veterans. If your family member or relative is eligible for veterans'

benefits, check with the VA or get in touch with the VA medical center nearest you. There could be a waiting list for VA nursing homes. To learn more about VA healthcare benefits, call 1-877-222-8387 or visit the Veterans Health Administration.

- **Social Security Administration (SSI) Program.** SSI is another program that provides monthly payments to adults aged 65 and older who have a disability. To qualify, your income and resources must be under certain limits. To find out more about these programs, call 1-800-772-1213 or TTY 1-800-325-0778, or visit the Social Security Administration in person.

- **National Council on Aging (NCOA).** The NCOA—a private group—has a free service called Benefits Checkup. This service can help you find federal and state benefit programs that may help your family. After providing some general information about the person who needs care, you can see a list of possible benefit programs to explore. Those programs can help pay for prescription drugs, heating bills, housing, meal programs, and legal services. You don't have to give a name, address, or social security number to use this service. To learn more about Benefits Checkup, visit benefitscheckup.org or call 1-571-527-3900.

As you can see, financing care for your aging loved one is a major component in the quality of their life and, more importantly, your life as a caregiver. This chapter merely gives you an overview of things to consider. It may be wise to discuss all matters related to finances with a financial manager. They can explain your options so that you can make a sound decision that is in the best interest of your loved one…and yourself.

Chapter 3
Handling Business

"Growing old is like climbing a mountain; you get a little out of breath, but the view is much better!"
~Ingrid Bergman ~

Just because your loved one has aged does not mean the day-to-day tasks of living life have stopped. The same things you deal with while managing your life, you may now have to add on the additional tasks of someone else. The following are some helpful tips for handling the affairs of daily living for your elderly loved one.

1. **Scheduling Appointments.** No matter your age, running errands and making appointments can be a hassle. When you are elderly, however, what might have once been a relatively minor aggravation or inconvenience can quickly grow into a nearly insurmountable obstacle.

    That is especially true for seniors who may have difficulties with memory or who may no longer be able to drive, yet the ability to run errands and keep appointments is an inevitable requirement of daily life. The good news, though, is that there are things you can do to help make those necessary chores easier for the seniors in your life.

a. **Why it Matters**. When you are caring for a senior loved one—whether they're living with you or still residing in their own home—there are many things to think about, from ensuring their safety while at home to making sure they're eating well and taking their medication. When you combine caregiving with the other daily obligations you must meet, planning for how you might make your senior's errands easier can fall fairly low on the priority list. The reality is that, without a plan, important needs may go unmet, which can take a profound toll on your senior's mental and physical well-being.

For example, if your loved one has mobility issues, they may delay necessary dental appointments, particularly if driving to the clinic or even accessing the dental chair is a challenge. Similarly, seniors who have memory or cognitive challenges may not remember to keep up with their oral care. Nevertheless, such care is essential, not only for ensuring good oral health, but also for protecting against conditions that can be related to oral disease, including an increased risk of heart disease, infections, and dementia. To ease some of the burdens of remembering those appointments and to incentivize seniors who may be reluctant to keep up with their oral care, it's a good idea to go ahead and schedule your seniors for their oral checkups and dental cleaning. Helping your loved one with the scheduling of essential medical and dental appointments can be particularly challenging in the face of the ongoing and worsening shortage of healthcare providers worldwide. Because of that, your loved one may need to seek alternative forms of medical care, such as turning to a Family Nurse Practitioner (FNP), who will generally be able to provide many of the same services as a General Practitioner or Primary Care Physician. If your senior has cognitive challenges, though, they may need your assistance with finding and booking an appointment with a qualified FNP.

2. **Managing the Logistics.** Scheduling and keeping track of your loved one's appointments will only be a first step in helping to make their errands and appointments easier. You will also want to help your loved one manage the logistics of the errand. If your senior lives on their own, for example, you might help them with remembering appointments by creating a schedule that can be posted in an accessible area of the home, such as on the refrigerator. As an added layer of support, you might schedule automatic reminders to be sent to their

email and/or smartphone. An array of apps can be downloaded at low or no cost to precisely do that.

In addition to making appointments and arranging reminders, you can also make the tasks easier for your seniors by ensuring they have both reliable transportation to their appointments and assistance with getting ready for them. That is especially important if your senior has difficulty with memory, mobility, or driving. Reputable caregivers can be hired to help your seniors manage their errands and appointments. For instance, caregivers can help your senior bathe and dress for a doctor's appointment, as well as drive them to it. For other errands, such as grocery shopping, prescription refills, or even pet care, a hired caregiver can often take care of those tasks for your senior. This can be a particularly important option in circumstances where your loved one may not feel well enough to leave the house themselves.

The Takeaway

Errands and appointments are a part of life. For the elderly, they can be formidably challenging, to the point where it can lead seniors to miss the vital care and services they need. Fortunately, there are steps you can take to make those daily chores easier for your senior, including scheduling necessary medical and dental appointments and creating timely appointment reminders. You can also help manage the logistics of an errand, including arranging for transportation and ensuring that your senior has the assistance needed to prepare for the appointment. Hired caregivers can even take care of some errands, such as food shopping, when your senior cannot or prefers not to leave home.

3. **Meals and Meal Planning.** Eating healthily and having an active lifestyle can support healthy aging. Simple adjustments can go a long way toward building a healthier eating pattern. Follow these tips to get the most out of food and beverages while meeting your loved one's nutritional needs and reducing the risk of disease.

    a. Provide a variety of foods from each food group to help reduce the risk of developing diseases such as high blood pressure, diabetes, and heart disease. Choose foods with little to no added sugar, saturated fats, and sodium.

    b. To get adequate protein throughout the day and maintain muscle, try adding seafood, dairy, and fortified soy products, along with beans, peas, and lentils to meals.

    c. Add sliced or chopped fruits and vegetables to meals and snacks. For your convenience, look for precut varieties if slicing and chopping are a challenge.

d. Try foods fortified with vitamin B12, such as some cereals, or talk to your elder's doctor about taking a B12 supplement.
   e. Reduce sodium intake by seasoning foods with natural herbs and citrus, such as lemon juice.
   f. Give them plenty of water throughout the day to help them stay hydrated and aid in the digestion of food and absorption of nutrients. Avoid sugary drinks.
4. **Meal Planning.** Meal planning for your elderly loved one should not become a burden that leaves you baffled and frustrated. In fact, when you have the correct information and motivation, you can feel good about making healthy choices. Use the following tips to plan healthy and delicious meals.
   a. **Plan in advance.** Meal planning takes the guesswork out of eating and can help ensure your loved one eats a variety of nutritious foods throughout the day.
   b. **Find budget-friendly foods.** Create a shopping list in advance to help stick to a budget. Be sure to include your elderly loved one in the planning. It's a waste of time to plan and prepare meals they will not eat.
   c. **Consider preparation time.** Some meals can be made in as little as five minutes. If you love

cooking or preparing a meal with or for family and friends, you may want to try something a little more challenging.

d. **Keep calories in mind.** The number of calories needed each day varies by individual. Always discuss their weight and overall fitness with their healthcare provider before making big changes.

5. **Prescription Medication Management.** As we age, our bodies change. Some changes, we can see and feel, including aches and pains that linger. Simple movements, like walking or getting out of a chair, may be slower or more painful than they used to be. Other changes we can't feel, including how our bodies may respond to and absorb the medicine. As a result, medicines will stay in the body longer, which can cause more severe side effects. Doses must be properly adjusted and monitored. Because of the changes in our bodies as we age, there is also a higher risk of drug interactions in older adults. Important factors to consider include:

- **Seniors use more medicines**—prescription, over-the-counter, and supplements—than any other age group in the U.S.
- **Older adults often use multiple medicines,** increasing the risk of drug interactions and the potential for side effects.

- **The liver and kidneys may not work as well as when your older adult was younger.** Decreased functions can affect how medicine works and is absorbed, broken down, and removed from the body.
- **Medicines may stay in the body longer** and cause side effects if doses are not properly adjusted.
- **Age-related changes,** such as weight loss, decreased body fluid, and increased fatty tissue can alter the way drugs are distributed and concentrated in the body.
- **Increased sensitivity to medicines** is more common in older adults.
- **Impaired memory, hearing, and vision** make it difficult to understand and remember instructions, especially for those with complicated regimens. Many older Americans also face declining grip strength, mobility, and memory lapses—all of which can affect the ability to take medication as prescribed.
- **Older adults tend to receive prescriptions from different healthcare professionals,** making it difficult to track medicines and identify drug interactions, harmful doses, and ineffective medicines.

- **Chronic conditions, such as diabetes, high blood pressure, and arthritis** are more common in older adults and often require a complex medication regimen.
- **Older adults may not follow medication plans** because of forgetfulness, side effects, a perception that the medicine isn't working, or cost.

The good news is that many of the risks or challenges can be prevented if you are informed about safe and appropriate medication use and how to get the most from your medications. Here are some tips to prevent problems:

- **Be aware of your loved one's health conditions and medicines.** Talk with healthcare providers, read trustworthy websites, and join support groups.
- **Maintain a medication list** with:
    - Medication names, including OTCs, supplements, and herbal remedies.
    - Who prescribed each prescription?
    - The purpose of each medication and the symptoms it should treat.
    - How often and what dose of each?
    - Are refills needed? How often?
    - Update the list when you administer something new, if a medicine is stopped, or if the dosage changes. Medications should be reviewed with the

healthcare provider so that your loved one is receiving only those that are needed.
- Discuss allergies and problems you've witnessed with medications. Never stop administering prescriptions without first checking with physicians.

- **Read the Drug Facts label, package inserts, and Patient Medicine Information leaflets,** which tell you:
  - What the medicine is for.
  - How to take the medicine.
  - How often it should be taken and the dosage.
  - Side effects or allergic reactions.
  - Warnings, including who shouldn't take the medicine, when to stop use and ask a doctor, and who is at increased risk of side effects.
  - Storage instructions.
- **Use one pharmacy** so that the pharmacist can monitor all medications and check for drug interactions.
- **Safely store medications.** Check expiration dates. Keep medicines in the bottle/tube they came in so that dosage and directions are at hand. Keep medicines up and away from children. Never share prescriptions or take others' medications.
- **Contact their provider immediately** if you notice problems with your loved one's medicine.

- **Identify a "patient navigator."** Ask their primary care physician to act as a "navigator" for the healthcare system so that one person/practice can ensure all conditions and treatment regimens are tracked. Medicare's Medication Therapy Management Program helps healthcare professionals fulfill that role.
6. **Ordering Supplies and Medical Equipment.** Choosing the correct medical supplies starts with properly outfitting your bathroom, home, and car emergency kit with first-aid basics and then supplementing them with products to manage any specific health needs. Too often, essentials aren't replaced after being used up, and a minor cut or burn causes panic because simple home medical supplies aren't available. Stocking up on medical supplies online means you're prepared for accidents and minor illnesses, as well as better health management for your elderly loved one.
    - **Everyday Essentials to Have on Hand:**
        - Bandages cover and protect a cut or other wound. Be sure you have a full complement of first-aid items, including self-adherent wraps, gauze rolls, surgical tape, and a variety of sizes of sterile bandages.

- Ointments and cleansers speed relief and help prevent further damage by giving a layer of protection.
- Topical painkillers include sprays or ointments for joint and muscle relief.
- Disinfecting wipes prevent the spread of germs at home, when traveling, or while in the hospital.
- Antibacterial skin cleansers prevent the spread of germs in everyday situations.
- Nutrition can include meal replacements or snacks that provide needed protein or simply extra calories over the course of the day. Depending on the formula, it's one way to consume needed vitamins and minerals.
- Compression socks help with circulation and are available in different tensions.
- Cold packs provide immediate pain relief and help prevent swelling. Heat pads provide soothing later in the case of an acute injury and on a regular basis for a chronic one.

• **Medical supplies** also include devices that allow you to better manage specific medical conditions at home. Once you have buying guidelines from your medical team, you can choose the correct home medical supplies online to be sure you have all recommended items.

- Catheters are used to manage certain urinary health conditions, including some forms of incontinence.
- Cervical collars and neck braces may be prescribed for rehab after surgery or injury.
- Electrotherapy and TENS home units are similar to the electrical nerve and muscle stimulation devices used by physical therapists for pain relief.
- Exam gloves protect against germs and are available in latex and latex-free, powdered and powder-free, and come in a range of sizes. They can be important safeguards when caring for someone with incontinence.
- Respiratory care products help people breathe easier every day. For allergies and other conditions, consider an air purifier or humidifier to make your home environment less irritating. Medical devices, such as nebulizers and oxygen concentrators, which deliver oxygen to

people with serious respiratory conditions, should be selected with their doctor's guidelines in mind.
- Edema pumps offer at-home treatments for people with circulatory problems.
- Oral swabs, such as Lemon Glycerin Swabsticks by Medline, help alleviate dry mouth conditions.

As a caregiver, it is especially important to check on medical supplies in your loved one's home and to properly outfit them if they downsize to a new home or senior residence.

7. **Hiring Home Healthcare Aides.** Home healthcare is comprised of a wide range of healthcare services that can be provided in your home for an illness or injury. Home healthcare is usually less expensive, more convenient, and just as effective as the care received in a hospital or Skilled Nursing Facility (SNF). Whether your loved one is aging in their home or living with you or a relative, hiring a home health aide is essential to the overall health and welfare of them and the caregiver.

    Aging in place means your loved one stays in the comfort of a home environment for as long as possible, rather than moving into a retirement or long-term care facility. Aging in place may be a viable option if your loved one only needs minor assistance with their daily activities, enjoy a close network of family and friends nearby, and can utilize the right home care services to cover their needs. By exploring the range of services available, you can decide if aging in place is the best option for you and your loved one to maintain their independence and be able to make the most of their golden years. Home healthcare services can include:

- Wound care for pressure sores or a surgical wound
- Patient and caregiver education
- Intravenous or nutrition therapy
- Injections
- Monitoring serious illness and unstable health status
- Mental healthcare
- Dental care
- Laboratory and diagnostic care
- Substance abuse treatment
- Preventative care
- Physical and occupational therapy
- Nutritional support
- Pharmaceutical care

In general, the goal of home healthcare is to treat an illness or injury. Home healthcare helps your elderly loved one:

- Get better
- Regain their independence

- Become as self-sufficient as possible
- Maintain their current condition or level of function
- Slow their physical decline

If your loved one receives Medicare benefits through a Medicare health plan, check with their plan to find out what their Medicare-covered home health benefits are. If there is a Medicare Supplement Insurance (Medigap) policy or other health insurance coverage, inform their doctor or other healthcare providers so that any bills get paid correctly. If their doctor or referring healthcare provider decides home healthcare is needed, they should give you a list of agencies that serve your area. They must tell you whether their organization has a financial interest in any agency listed.

So, what should you expect from a home healthcare provider? Here are some examples of what the home health staff should be doing:

- Check what your loved one is eating and drinking.
- Check blood pressure, temperature, heart rate, and breathing.
- Check that all prescriptions, other drugs, and any treatments are being taken correctly.
- Monitor pain levels.
- Check safety in the home.
- Coordinate their care. That means they must communicate regularly with you, their doctor,

and anyone else who provides care. I suggest maintaining a written log of everything pertaining to the care of your loved one and making it available to all parties concerned.

The range of home healthcare services a patient can receive at home is limitless. Depending on the individual patient's situation, care can range from nursing care to specialized medical services, such as laboratory workups. You and your elderly loved one's doctor will determine the best care plan and services that might be needed at home.

8. **Living Arrangements.** One of the most important decisions to make for older adults is their choice of housing. Their future contentment, comfort, and even safety may depend on careful consideration of all the housing options available to them. Fortunately, an array of housing options and living arrangements can meet the needs of those who are aging. Understanding what the options are and the needs they fill are the first steps toward making wise decisions.

    - **Aging in Place.** Aging in place means staying in the comfort of their own home for as long as possible as your loved one gets older, rather than moving into a retirement or long-term care facility. Everyone's needs vary, depending on factors such as how much support is available, general health and mobility, and their financial situation. Here are some of the issues to consider when evaluating aging in place and home care options:

- **Location and accessibility.** Where is their home located? Are your loved ones in a rural or suburban area that requires a lot of driving? If they're in an area with more public transportation, is it safe and easily accessible?
- **Home accessibility/maintenance.** Is their home easily modified? Does it have a lot of steps or a steep hill to access? Do they have a large yard that needs to be maintained?
- **Available support.** Do they have family and friends nearby? How involved are they? Are they able to provide your loved one with the support needed?
- **Medical conditions.** No one can predict the future. However, if your elderly loved one has a chronic medical condition that is expected to worsen over time, it's especially important to think about how health and mobility problems will be handled. What are common complications

of their condition, and how will they be handled?

- **Senior Community/Assisted Living Facility.** If you are new to the world of senior housing, you probably imagine all the options for senior living as the same: they are "nursing" or "retirement" homes. In reality, there are many kinds of senior housing, all with their own features. Two of the most important differences are the independence levels of the residents and the type of care available for seniors at each type of facility.

Let's look at the differences between an assisted living facility and a retirement community.

  - **The Level of Care.** Residents in an assisted living facility need a higher level of care than those in a retirement community. Assisted living residents need daily assistance with one or more activities of daily living (ADLs), like managing medications, bathing, dressing, driving, arranging transportation, or managing household chores. Three meals a day are provided, and the facility is staffed 24/7 with employees, including medical staff, ready to help residents when the need arises. Transportation, housekeeping, and laundry services are most likely all provided.

Likewise, retirement community residents don't need as much care as assisted living residents. You may also hear retirement communities referred to as "independent living communities." That means the seniors who live there don't need the level of care and help with ADLs that assisted living residents do. A retirement community is designed for seniors (some are age-restricted to 55 and up) who can generally care for themselves. Seniors may move to a retirement community when they just need the low-hassle lifestyle of a low-maintenance apartment or condo, want the convenience of on-site dining and entertainment, or even just want to live around people with similar interests and take advantage of the sense of community.

- **The Staff.** Assisted living facilities are not regulated by federal or state governments, so there are no strict rules about how they must be staffed. However, most large, assisted living facilities employ some registered nurses full time, and smaller facilities hire visiting nurses or part-time registered nurses to supervise nurse assistants. The certified nursing assistants (CNAs) and medical assistants provide most of the care to residents. A retirement community, or independent living facility, probably won't have medical professionals on site all the time. A community like this, however, will employ security staff, and you will be able to contact them about a medical or security emergency at any time.

- **The Cost.** In general, the more care a resident needs, the higher the cost. Assisted living, with its available services like help with ADLs, three meals a day, laundry, housekeeping, and 24/7 medical staff, will cost more than an independent living retirement community. Accordingly, based on a 2020 Cost of Care Survey, the average monthly cost of an assisted living facility in the United States is $4,300, which equals $51,600 per year. It must be noted that the cost varies depending on what part of the country one resides in and the facility itself. Retirement community costs vary even more, depending on where you live and the amenities offered by the facility. They can start as low as $1,500 a month but can get as high as $6,000 monthly (roughly $18,000 to $72,000 yearly). If the retirement community is a CCRC, there will also be a one-time admission fee when you first move in. The fee can be hefty, but the average entrance fee is $329,000.

- **Living with Children.** "Shared living"—when adults live under the same roof but are not romantically involved—is on the upswing. A major factor in the trend is parents moving in with their adult children, which is a twist on the "boomerang" phenomenon of young adults moving in with their parents. If you decide to move an elderly parent or other aging relative in with you, you won't be alone. One out of every four caregivers lives with an elderly or disabled loved one whom he or she cares for, but it's not the best option for everyone. It may be cheaper than putting the person in a nursing home (which costs about $80,000 per year on average) or an assisted living facility (about $43,000 per year on average), but you could pay a heavy price in terms of time, stress, fatigue, and strained relations. Consider the following questions before choosing this option:

- **What kind of care will they need?** What is the person's physical and mental condition? What chronic illness does he or she have? Those are the first questions you need to answer. Most people don't consider caring for an elderly parent in their own home until a health setback or crisis comes into play. In that case, it's very likely you will be coping with the person's chronic illness. Even if an aging family member is just slowing down without an illness such as Alzheimer's or cancer to deal with, you still need to anticipate your loved one's future condition based on family and personal history.
- **How much assistance and supervision can you give?** Caring for an aging relative is a great way to give back some of the love, care, and nurturing they gave to you, and it provides a model for your children that shows them what caring and commitment are about. However, you

must be realistic about your limits, schedule, and availability.

- **How well do you get along?** Look at the history of your relationship with your family member. If you enjoy each other's company and can successfully resolve your differences, that's a real plus. That doesn't mean you can never argue or have to be best friends. All families have some conflict. If both of you can get over it quickly or simply agree to disagree, then you've already done much of the groundwork. If the two of you have never really gotten along, don't expect the relationship to change magically now. You may feel you're doing the right thing, but if you're both going to be miserable, it's probably wiser to pursue other options first.
- **Will they contribute financially?** A major consideration is the financial resources available from your elderly loved one to contribute to the overall finances to provide care for them. If you move someone in, it will probably cost you—both in dollars and lifestyle. A recent study by

the National Alliance for Caregiving (NAC) and Evercare found that caregivers spend on average about $5,500 a year out of pocket to care for an aging relative. How do people afford it? The study found that most make sacrifices elsewhere. Almost half cut back on vacations and leisure activities, one-third dip into savings, and one-quarter cut back on groceries and spending for their own health or dental care to help pay for their aging parent's care.

- **How do your spouse and children feel about the move in?** Children need to be prepared for the extra chores that might be necessary to take care of their grandparents and to relinquish some of the spotlight, since their needs will now sometimes take a back seat. A child may have to give up their bedroom or share it with a sibling or older adult and may need help adapting to the new living situation. Do your spouse and other family members get along, or do they bicker? An older adult who's in decent health may not require a lot of attention, but if they need a lot of help and supervision, you and your spouse will have a lot less alone time, and your social lives may be put on hold. Make sure you're both prepared for the sacrifice before proceeding.

9. **Money Management.** As one retires, they finally get the free time they've always wanted to enjoy their golden years. However, living a retired life comes with its own set of challenges, with the biggest one probably being the lack of sufficient income. Many people may get a pension during their old age, but that is not true for everyone. Even then, managing to live on a fixed pension is also something that needs some effort. The following are some basic tips for money management that can go a long way in helping you to help your senior loved one sort out their finances:

    - **Track expenses and create a budget.** One of the best budgeting tips is to be realistic with the budget. Unless they have planned very carefully in their early years, retirement income will most likely not be equal to their income during peak earning years. That is why limiting present expenses is the best financial advice for the elderly, as a tight comprehensive budget will allow you to help them maximize their retirement corpus. Another important tip for money management is to monitor the budget and stay on track.

- **Automate financial tasks.** One of the top financial tips that can make your life easier is to automate your loved one's finances to streamline them. Automate all their income from pension funds and other sources and direct them toward any payments or investments that need to be made. Arrange for all their regular bills and payments to be directly debited from their account on the day that suits you best. Make sure you have a buffer zone in the plan so that even if an expected income is delayed due to any reason, you don't have to worry about pending payments. Whoever is responsible for your elder's finances (as outlined in Chapter 2) must be vigilant in overseeing this task.

- **Power of Attorney.** A good tip for money management is to establish a Power of Attorney. It can be quite important. A Power of Attorney allows you or one of your family members to manage your elderly loved one's financial affairs in a situation where they are unable to do so. The Power of Attorney helps make certain that their wishes are respected while still alive but not in the right condition communicate them. Another important money management tip is to consider appointing more than one Power of Attorney to mitigate the risk of fraud.

- **Creating a will.** Although it's not a pleasant financial planning tip, it is still quite important. Facing your loved one's mortality is never easy, but making a will offers you peace of mind in knowing that any funds will be used and disbursed exactly as intended. A will also helps to eliminate any family drama that typically accompanies the death of an elderly loved one, especially if they managed to accumulate assets during their lifetime.

When it comes to the best financial tips, one size does not fit all. Every individual has varying needs as well as the capital they have saved. Seeking professional advice when it comes to money management tips is always a good idea, if needed.

Chapter 4
Emotional Daily Living

*"The body heals with play. The mind heals with laughter.
The spirit heals with joy."*
~ Proverb ~

As your parents age, they may feel useless, lonely, angry, or even in denial about their wellness and capabilities. Living alone may further exacerbate negative feelings. Emotional health is just as important as physical health for seniors, yet there's often more of an emphasis on physical needs rather than emotional ones when providing care. Overlooking emotional concerns can have a negative effect on overall health and well-being. Growing older isn't always easy. While there are benefits, such as increased freedom and the ability to retire, many seniors are faced with new challenges. Relationships change, social circles dwindle, and health problems may increase. As a senior's life evolves, so does his or her emotional needs.

What are the emotional needs of your elderly loved ones?

1. **Safety and Security.** The biggest fear for older adults is falling. It is bigger than robbery, financial stress, or health issues. Providing a safe, secure environment for older adults is crucial to their well-being. Regularly assess your aging parent's home for fall risks, such as

clutter. Check if they're locking their doors at night or install a home security system to ensure their safety. If your parents are living with you, you may have to add some features to ensure their safety.

   a. **Low-cost safety tips.** Many people find that they can make the changes themselves.
   i. Add textured, no-slip strips to the bathtub and shower.
   ii. Apply nonslip wax on floors.
   iii. Place a waterproof chair or bench in the shower.
   iv. Put nonskid treads on steps.
   v. Remove throw rugs.
   vi. Remove wheels on chairs.
   vii. Replace standard doorknobs with level handles.
   viii. Replace toilet with a raised or high-profile toilet.
   ix. Use rubber-backed bathmats.

   b. **Costly changes.** The following modifications often require professional help to make a home more accessible for a wheelchair:
   i. Alter the shower for walk-in rather than step-over entry.
   ii. Create zero-threshold entryways.

iii. Move light switches for easy reach from a wheelchair or bed.
iv. Widen doorways and hallways.

2. **Connection/Social Interaction.** When you go to work every day, you probably see familiar faces, say hello to your favorite coworkers, and eat lunch with at least one or two regulars. You might talk about last night's game, a new recipe you discovered, or share tidbits of your life. Then comes retirement, and you no longer have a familiar routine. You're free to do whatever you want, yet with that freedom often comes loneliness. It's too easy for seniors to stay at home and spend more time alone, especially as their mobility decreases. People need connection, no matter their age. Feelings disconnected emotionally and physically from people can be detrimental to one's health. Due to COVID-19, 56% of older adults reported feeling isolated with infrequent social interaction. Senior isolation has been shown to increase the risk for all the following:
    a. Depression
    b. Anxiety
    c. Cognitive decline
    d. Dementia
    e. Long-term illness
    f. High blood pressure
    g. Mortality

h. Alcoholism
i. Drug abuse
j. Susceptibility to fraud and other forms of elder abuse

To properly combat senior isolation, you should encourage social activity as part of your loved one's elderly care program. There are all sorts of ways you can encourage social activity for your loved one.

- **Increase your time with them.** If you can, increase the amount of time you spend visiting and interacting with your loved one. Frequent short visits are better than infrequent long visits, and regular phone calls can help when you're unable to be there in person.
- **Encourage the family to visit.** Express your concerns to other family members. Encourage them to visit and become involved with your loved one's elderly care.
- **Consider an animal companion.** So long as your loved one can care for a pet, a new animal companion like a cat or dog can make a world of difference to feelings of loneliness.
- **Suggest visiting and hosting friends.** If your loved one seems to be turning away from the world, encourage them to reach out to friends for visits and get-togethers.

- **Encourage outside activities.** Have your loved one join you on trips to the grocery store, afternoons at the movies, and other activities that get them out of the home.
- **Suggest joining a club or volunteering.** Group activities, such as a book club, bridge club, or senior fitness class can be a great way to promote social interaction. You might also want to suggest volunteering with an organization like your local church, theater, or library.
- **Companion Care services.** One of the elderly care services offered by many home health agencies is Companion Care. This service provides your loved one with regular visits from an agency companion.

As the senior population grows, the negative health effects of isolation will likely become an even bigger problem. Addressing the causes of isolation with your senior loved one can increase their physical health and emotional well-being. By helping your loved one find outlets for socialization, it is possible to extend longevity and independence while reducing overall medical expenses.

3. **Autonomy.** It is a parent's responsibility to take care of a child—to see that their needs are met and that they feel safe and secure. With aging parents, those traditional

roles often reverse. Many seniors have difficulty leaning on their children for support as they get older. They may feel uncomfortable or even embarrassed asking for help, relying on you to take care of daily tasks, or do not want to change your relationship with them. Your elderly loved one has been independent their whole adult life. As such, growing old and relying on others can be a tough transition for them. In-home caregivers are a great option for older adults who want to retain independence but need regular care. An in-home caregiver fulfills the emotional needs of elderly people and their physical needs, such as meal preparation, bathing, dressing, etc.

How to take care of the emotional needs of your elderly loved ones?

Elderly people need to feel safe and should be surrounded by familiar faces. Coping with emotional needs prevents aging people from depression. Signs of depression include insufficient sleeping patterns, poor appetite, and unstable concentration. Every emotional care offered to seniors should be designed in a way that deals with loneliness, boredom, vulnerability, and isolation.

So, how do we take care of the emotional needs of elderly people?

1. **Planning.** Anticipate changes. The circumstances will never remain the same; hence, your elderly loved one is certain to face new difficulties in physical, sensory, and emotional abilities. Over a period, you may notice some of the following symptoms that you must address:
    - **Denial.** Some older people cope by refusing to acknowledge changes have occurred in themselves. They may decide to ignore change and hope it goes away by itself.
    - **Loneliness.** The older person might isolate themselves as a way of mourning the loss of familiar people and (possibly) their spouse.
    - **Sense of helplessness.** Some older people might feel they are so useless, helpless, and at the mercy of their physical problems, changes in living arrangements, or negative events.
    - **Grief.** Grief is a normal reaction to the loss of a loved one, former lifestyle, relationships, health, vision and hearing, capability level, mobility, or independence.
    - **Anger/Rage.** When older people feel they have no control over the present, they may react by showing their anger. They may release their anger towards their family members who are most supportive because they know those people will still love them despite their anger.

Those changes can brutally damage the emotional well-being of the loved one and caregiver. If you are providing home care service, you should look out for mood alterations and their immediate response.

2. **Recreational Activities.** Aging in today's world no longer means retiring to a rocking chair to watch TV and occasionally play Bingo. Seniors want adventure, plenty of stimulation, and a chance to learn something new. Indeed, most seniors residing in assisted living facilities find that they have many more opportunities for engagement than they ever had at home. Understand the needs of your elderly loved ones. Talk to them, listen carefully to their needs, and discuss activities they are interested in. Check out the following great options, which you may find at your local senior living community:

    - **Group Exercise Class.** Group exercises, like yoga or Tai-Chi, are fun and sociable ways to improve flexibility and balance, which are key to preventing falls in older adults. Some communities offer chair exercise classes, while others may offer water aerobics programs, which can appeal to seniors who are living with arthritis.
    - **Wii Sports.** The senior in your life may not be able to shoot basketballs anymore, but

Nintendo Wii's interactive console games, in which you move your body instead of pressing buttons or using a joystick, offer a nice alternative. There are a variety of games that sports-minded seniors can play, including bowling, tennis, golf, and the aforementioned basketball.

- **Gardening Club.** Gardening is a superb way to go outside, stay active, and remain connected to others. Digging in the dirt and planting and weeding can help seniors relax and unwind. Not only that, but they also get to reap the benefits of their labor: beautiful flowers or tasty veggies!
- **Book Club.** If the senior in your life is an avid reader, chances are they'd love the opportunity to share their opinion about a book with others. Not only do book clubs support seniors' efforts to stay sharp, mentally alert, and in touch with the world, but they also have a huge social element.
- **Spa Days and Self-Care.** Everyone knows that self-care is essential. Its value doesn't end during one's senior years. Many senior living communities offer special spa days—including

haircuts, manicures, and even skin treatments—to foster well-being.

Every senior deserves a chance to relax, learn something new, and enjoy the retirement they've worked so hard for. There are exceptional senior living facilities and communities that honor seniors for who they are, while helping them work to become who they want to be. Retirement should mark the beginning of an exciting new life chapter, whether your loved ones are living on their own, with you, or in a senior living facility.

3. **Connecting with family and friends.** Assist your elderly loved ones with connecting with their close friends. Encourage visits to family members and make regular use of telecommunication to maintain regular communication. Elderly people may find internet access useful; hence, we can also teach them the usage of technology.

Benefits of technology for the elderly.

- **Social connection.** Various technologies allow your loved ones to catch up with family. They can use Skype and FaceTime to talk to their grandchildren or email to send an instant letter to a friend. Facebook, Twitter, Instagram, and other social media platforms can be used to see what people are up to and share thoughts or pictures.

- **Mental stimulation.** Learning to master new technology can provide mental stimulation and may protect your loved one's brain against disease.
- **Safety.** Medical alert systems and cell phones can be life-saving technologies to have on hand in an emergency. Technology has also provided advancements in the medical field—from cell phone apps that can remind seniors to take their medications to doctors' offices that use online programs to store medical data and coordinate care.
- **Exercise and fun.** One can find a host of exercise videos online, depending on their activity level. Engaging with video games can encourage your elderly loved one to get up and move. Whatever their hobbies may be, there probably is a technology that exists to allow them to explore their interests in greater depth.
- **How to introduce technology to your senior adult.** No matter how you decide to bring your family member on board with technology, be sensitive to your loved one's needs and patient with them as they grasp new concepts.
- **Help to build confidence slowly.** Many older adults get frustrated when using technology. Sometimes, when they are being taught, the instructor goes "too fast," so the senior becomes

discouraged about their ability to learn. If you are teaching your loved one, start slowly and let them know they can do it!

- **Begin with easy tasks.** Actions, such as how to view pictures or the basics of swiping and scrolling on the screen, are good starting points when teaching how to use technology.
- **Share the benefits of using technology.** Let your family member know about all the great things they can do with technology. Emphasize the ways it can make their life easier and more fun once they understand how to use it.
- **Get your loved one connected.** Purchasing a tablet and securing an internet connection for your family member is an excellent place to start as you get them set up for accessing technology.

When it comes to using technology, there is a world of benefits to explore. If your senior loved one is ready to check out how technology can help them stay connected to family and friends, it will open a brand-new world for them.

4. **Grooming.** To retain dignity and feelings of self-worth, it is important to foster a good care regimen. When working on personal care, the first thing that strikes us is grooming, but there are several factors involved. Assisting senior citizens in their daily work fosters a feeling of respect. Let's discuss tips for assisting senior

people with bathing, dressing, oral hygiene, and grooming.

- **Bathing.** When it comes to hygiene, regular bathing is perhaps the most important action one can take to ensure their hygiene is up to par. Unfortunately, assisting elderly people with bathing can be quite cumbersome and difficult if you are not aware of some common issues and overlooked aspects. Here are some helpful considerations:
  - Allow the elderly person to perform shower/bathing steps on their own if they can. Avoid micro-management and give simple instructions when needed.
  - Try to perform bathing and other hygienic chores at the same time each day, taking care to follow the same routine each time. Doing so can help make bathing go more quickly and smoothly. That also applies to post-bathing routines, such as drying off.
  - Install any necessary grab bars and railings in the shower and bath, as well as non-slip inserts on the floors of the shower and bath. Install any other helpful equipment, such as a bench in the shower, as needed.

- It is highly advisable that locks be removed from the doors of bathrooms. If an emergency occurs while the elderly person is in the bathroom alone, they can call out for help and the respondent can quickly gain entry.
- Make sure the bathroom and shower/tub areas have adequate lighting.
  Taking the time to make sure all necessary items and equipment needed for showering and bathing are on hand prior to performing either task can make the time go more smoothly. Be sure you consider the needs and wants of your elderly loved one.
- **Dressing your elderly loved one.** Getting dressed is a daily action that most of us take for granted. We often don't think twice about putting our arms up to dive into a sweater or reaching down to tie our shoes. In caregiving situations, your elderly loved one may have lost the ability to dress themselves and may need help. Sometimes, that can cause challenging situations.

Many older adults prefer being dressed in daytime clothes each day. Being dressed often helps them feel more confident and comfortable when interacting with others. For many caregivers, helping someone dress and undress twice a day can be mentally and physically exhausting. To help the process run more smoothly, here are some helpful tips for those who are helping an older adult with dressing:

- **Allow extra time for dressing.** Allowing plenty of time each day for dressing and undressing helps the process feel more relaxed, calm, and pleasant. That makes it more likely that your older adult will cooperate and help with the process. Because of common health conditions, it usually takes a lot of extra time to help older adults get dressed. For example, if your older adult has cognitive impairments like Alzheimer's or dementia, they may not be able to sequence the steps of getting dressed or understand how a clothing item is worn. If your older adult has lost flexibility, mobility, hand dexterity, or is recovering from a stroke or surgery, they may need to move slowly through the dressing steps to avoid pain.
- **Give simple choices.** No matter a person's age or cognitive ability, people like to have a choice in what they wear. Providing two or three appropriate, seasonal options helps elderly loved ones maintain a sense of self and control through the act of choosing what to wear.
- **Check for skin issues.** While you help someone get dressed, it also gives you a chance to check for any skin issues so that you can help them stay as healthy and

comfortable as possible. Redness, irritation, and pressure sores can quickly develop in those who have limited mobility. Pay particular attention to the buttocks, shoulder blades, elbows, and heels. It's important to catch skin breakdown early to avoid open wounds and infections.

- **Reduce combative behaviors.** When someone has Alzheimer's or dementia, they may become combative when you try to help them dress or undress. Sometimes, changing your approach can help. Each person is different, so it's a good idea to try varying approaches or timing to see what works best for them. Some people may feel more comfortable if they see you approaching and helping with their clothes. If what you're doing isn't clearly visible to them, they might feel startled or scared. Others might feel defensive and get combative if you stand in front of them while helping them with dressing. If that's the case, try approaching from the side (out of their direct line of sight) and gently put your arm around them. That may help them feel less threatened by the dressing process—especially when a calm voice and gentle touch are used.

When you take these tips into consideration, assisting your aging loved one with basic daily tasks, like dressing, does not have to be a chore. Older adults, in general, want to look their best and not have to spend too much time getting ready in the morning. Using the right clothes, perhaps some assistive devices, and a patient spirit can help elderly adults dress faster and confidently to get on with their day.

5. **Oral Hygiene.** Having good oral hygiene, including taking care of your teeth and gums as you get older, can prevent problems like toothaches, tooth decay (cavities), and tooth loss. A healthy mouth also makes it easier for your elderly loved ones to eat well and enjoy food. That becomes especially important if there are health conditions present, such as diabetes or heart disease, or if medicines are being taken that can cause oral health problems. Here are some steps to follow as guidelines for healthier teeth and gums in the elderly:
    - Encourage elderly people to brush their teeth and dentures (if they have them) at least twice a day.
    - Make sure the elderly person you are assisting is visiting their dentist on a regular basis.
    - Regular dental checkups are even more important for seniors with dentures, as ill-fitting ones can result in mouth sores and lead to poor eating habits.
    - Watch for changes in the mouth. As we age, the chances of disease increase. You should take your elderly loved one to the dentist if you

spot any of the following symptoms for more than two weeks:
- A spot in their mouth, lip, or throat that feels uncomfortable or sore
- A lump or thick area in their mouth, lip, or throat
- A white or red patch in their mouth
- Trouble chewing, swallowing, or moving their jaw or tongue
- Numbness in their tongue or mouth
- Swelling in their jaw
- Pain in one ear without hearing loss

There's no single rule for how often people need to see the dentist, as it varies from person to person. The next time you take your loved one to get a checkup and cleaning, ask the dentist how often your loved one needs to be seen.

Keep in mind that Medicare alone doesn't cover most dental care, so you may want to get private dental insurance for your loved one. Most Medicare Advantage plans have dental coverage.

6. **Grooming.** The burden typically falls on the family to acknowledge the signs of decline that are associated with aging parents. Hence, they may want to facilitate daily living tasks. Poor personal hygiene may be common and sometimes the primary sign that a parent might need some help. That doesn't necessarily mean that your

beloved should go into assisted living or a nursing home. However, they may need some assistance. Grooming is among the several roles caregivers may have to assume.

- **Hair.** If the elderly person had a regular routine when it came to hair maintenance before they began to need grooming assistance, try to make it so that they can keep their original routine. When getting a haircut, be sure to get styles that are easy to maintain. If the elderly person's hair needs to be washed, it may be easier to wash it in the kitchen sink, especially if it has a hose or spray attachment, rather than using the tub or shower.

- **Shaving.** When it comes to assisting elderly people with grooming, shaving is perhaps one of the more difficult tasks to perform effectively. Let the elderly person shave themselves for as long as possible, with you simply acting in a supervisory capacity. You may find that an electric razor will help with getting rid of hair on the face and other areas of the body immensely. Plucking certain facial hairs may be more effective than shaving.

- **Nail care and maintenance.** Encourage seniors to take care of their nails by themselves for as long as they can. Some may find that nail maintenance is a much more enjoyable task while watching television or listening to music. When they begin to need assistance, try to trim their fingernails and toenails at least twice a month. Sometimes, toenails and other foot issues, such as bunions, can cause seniors to experience discomfort when walking. A visit to the podiatrist, which is covered by most health insurance plans, may be necessary.

- **Makeup.** Some elderly women may find that applying makeup becomes harder as each day goes by, until they simply stop applying it completely. You can help make elderly women who have given up on makeup feel better by assisting them with the application. Even some powder and light-toned lipstick can work wonders.

7. **Security.** A senior citizen may feel nervous and fearful. When residing alone, they must deal with several issues, such as lack of mobility. Give a positive outlook with practical measures to prevent intruders. Arrange or install CCTV cameras, locks, chains, or spy holes with emergency call buttons so that even if they feel unwell, they can immediately reach out to those closest to them.

Growing older isn't always easy. While there are benefits, such as increased freedom and the ability to retire, many seniors are faced with new challenges. Relationships change, social circles dwindle, and health problems may increase. As a senior's life evolves, so will their emotional needs. Do your best to be there for them through it all.

Chapter 5
Caregiver

"One person caring about another represents life's GREATEST value."
~ Jim Rohn ~

It is estimated that approximately 65 million is the number of family caregivers in the U.S. who, day in and day out, do the incredibly important but undervalued work of caring for aging loved ones or people with disabilities. Chances are, you're a caregiver or know someone who is. The work isn't easy. According to the National Alliance for Caregiving, family caregivers provide an average of 20 hours of care per week, with the majority caring for an aging loved one. For most, caregiving isn't limited to a few months or even a year. NAC's research found that caregiving lasts an average of almost five years.

So, what's involved in self-care for caregivers? Even the airlines instruct you to put on your oxygen mask before helping others!

1. **Taking care of yourself**
    a. **Effects of caregiving on your health and well-being.** "My significant other is the one with Alzheimer's, but now I'm the one in the hospital!" Have you ever heard that complaint? That situation is far too common. Researchers know a lot about the effects of caregiving on health and

well-being. The combination of prolonged stress, the physical demands of caregiving, and the biological vulnerabilities that come with age place you at risk for significant health problems. If you are a "baby boomer" who has assumed a caregiver role for your parents while simultaneously juggling work and raising adolescent children, you face an increased risk for depression, chronic illness, and a possible decline in quality of life.

b. **Taking responsibility for your own care.** You cannot stop the impact of a chronic or progressive illness or a debilitating injury on someone for whom you care, but there is a great deal you can do to take responsibility for your personal well-being and to get your own needs met.

c. **Identify personal barriers.** Many times, attitudes and beliefs form personal barriers that stand in the way of caring for yourself. Not taking care of yourself may be a lifelong pattern, with caring for others an easier option. However, as a family caregiver, you must ask yourself, "What good will I be to the person I care for if I become ill or die?" Breaking old patterns and overcoming obstacles is not an easy proposition, but it can be done—regardless of your age or situation. The first task in removing personal barriers to self-care is to identify what is in your way. For example:

　　i. Do you think you are being selfish if you put your needs first?
　　ii. Is it frightening to think of your own needs? What is that fear about?
　　iii. Do you have trouble asking for what you need? Do you feel inadequate if you ask for help?
　　iv. Do you feel you have to prove you are worthy of the care recipient's affection? Do you do too much as a result?

Caregivers sometimes have misconceptions that increase their stress and get in the way of good self-care. Here are some of the most commonly expressed:

- I am responsible for my parent's health.
- If I don't do it, no one will.
- If I do it right, I will get the love, attention, and respect I deserve.
- Our family always takes care of our own.
- I promised my father I would always take care of my mother.

Because we base our behavior on our thoughts and beliefs, attitudes and misconceptions like those noted above can cause caregivers to continually attempt to do what cannot be done and control what cannot be controlled. The result is feelings of continued failure, frustration, and often an inclination to ignore your own needs. Ask yourself what might be getting in your way and keeping you from taking care of yourself.

2. **Moving forward.** Once you've started to identify personal barriers to good self-care, you can begin to change your behavior, moving forward one small step at a time. Consider some of the following effective tools for self-care that can start you on your way:

   a. **Reducing personal stress.** The way you perceive and respond to an event is a significant factor in how you adjust and cope with it. The stress you feel is not only the result of your caregiving situation; it's also the result of your perception of it—whether you see the glass as half-full or half-empty. It is important to remember that you are not alone in your experiences. Your level of stress is influenced by many factors, including:

      i. **Whether your caregiving is voluntary.** If you feel you had no choice in taking on the responsibilities, the chances are even greater that you will experience strain, distress, and resentment.

ii. **Your relationship with the care recipient.** Sometimes, people care for another with the hope of healing a relationship. If healing does not occur, you may feel regret and disappointment.

iii. **Your coping abilities.** How you coped with stress in the past predicts how you will cope now. Identify your current coping strengths so that you can build on them.

iv. **Your caregiving situation.** Some caregiving situations are more stressful than others. For example, caring for a person with dementia is often more stressful than caring for someone with a physical limitation.

v. **Whether or not support is available.** Do you have support from other family members or friends?

b. **Steps to manage stress**

i. **Recognize warning signs early.** Warning signs might include irritability, sleep problems, and forgetfulness. Know your own warning signs and act to make changes. Don't wait until you are overwhelmed.

ii. **Identify sources of stress.** Ask yourself, "What is causing stress for me?" Sources of stress might be that you have too much to do, family disagreements, feelings of inadequacy, or the inability to say no.

iii. **Identify what you can and cannot change.** Remember: We can only change ourselves; we cannot change another person. When you try to change things you have no control over, you will only increase your sense of frustration. Ask yourself, "What do I have some control over? What can I change?" Even a small change can make a big difference.

iv. **Take action.** Taking some action to reduce stress gives us back a sense of control. Stress reducers can be simple activities like walking and other forms of exercise, gardening, meditation, or having coffee with a friend. Identify some stress reducers that work for you.

3. **Setting goals.** Setting goals or deciding what you would like to accomplish in the next three to six months is an

important tool for taking care of yourself. Here are some simple goals you might set:

    a. Take a break from caregiving.

    b. Get help with caregiving tasks, such as bathing and preparing meals.

    c. Engage in activities that will make you feel healthier.

Goals are generally too big to work on all at once. We are more likely to reach a goal if we break it down into smaller action steps. Once you've set a goal, ask yourself, "What steps do I take to reach my goal?" Make an action plan by deciding which step you will take first and when.

Then, get started!

4. **Seeking solutions.** Seeking solutions to difficult situations is, of course, one of the most important tools in caregiving. Once you've identified a problem, taking action to solve it can change the situation and attitude to a more positive one, giving you more confidence in your abilities. Here are some suggested steps for seeking solutions:

    a. **Identify the problem.** Look at the situation with an open mind. The real problem might not be what first comes to mind. For example, you think the problem is simply that you are tired all the time, when the more basic difficulty is your belief that "no one can care for my loved one like

I can." The problem here is thinking that you must do everything yourself.

b. **List possible solutions.** One idea is to try a different perspective. "Even though someone else provides help to my loved one in a different way than I do, it can be just as good." Ask a friend to help.

c. **Select one solution from your list.** Then, try it!

d. **Evaluate the results.** Ask yourself, "How well did my choice work?"

e. **Try a second solution.** If your first idea didn't work, select another—but don't give up on the first. Sometimes, an idea just needs fine-tuning.

f. **Use other resources.** Ask family members, friends, and professionals for suggestions.

g. **If nothing seems to work,** accept that the problem may not be solvable now. You can revisit it at another time.

<u>*Note:*</u> All too often, we jump from the first to the last step and then feel defeated and stuck. Concentrate on keeping an open mind while listing and experimenting with possible solutions.

5. **Asking for and accepting help.** When people have asked if they can be of help to you, how often have you replied, "Thank you, but I'm fine"? Many caregivers

don't know how to marshal the goodwill of others and are reluctant to ask for help. You may not wish to "burden" others or admit that you can't handle everything yourself.

Be prepared with a mental list of ways that others can help you. For example, someone could take the person you care for on a 15-minute walk a couple of times a week. Your neighbor could pick up a few things for you at the grocery store. A relative could fill out some insurance paperwork. When you break down the jobs into very simple tasks, it is easier for people to help—and they truly want to help. It is up to you to tell them how. Help can come from community resources, family, friends, and professionals. Ask them. Don't wait until you are overwhelmed and exhausted or your health fails. Reaching out for help when you need it is a sign of personal strength. Asking for help is not easy for everyone. Here are some tips to help you ask:

a. **Consider the person's special abilities and interests.** If you know a friend who enjoys cooking but dislikes driving, your chances of getting help improve if you ask for help with meal preparation.

b. **Resist asking the same person repeatedly.** Do you keep asking the same person because they have trouble saying no?

c. **Pick the best time to make a request.** Timing is important. A person who is tired and stressed might not be available to help. Wait for a better time.

d. **Prepare a list of things that need to be done.** The list might include errands, yard work, or a visit with your loved one while you take a break. Let the "helper" choose what they would like to do.

e. **Be prepared for hesitancy or refusal.** It can be upsetting for the caregiver when a person is unable or unwilling to help. In the long run, it will do more harm to the relationship if the person helps only because they don't want to upset you. To the person who seems hesitant, simply say, "Why don't you think about it?" Try not to take it personally when a request is turned down. The person is turning down the task, not you. Try not to let a refusal prevent you from asking for help again. The person who refused today may be happy to help at another time.

f. **Avoid weakening your request.** "It's only a thought, but would you mind staying with Grandma while I went to church?" The request sounds like it's not very important to you. Use "I" statements to make specific requests. "I would like to go to church on Sunday. Would you stay with Grandma from 9 a.m. until noon?"

    g. **The answer will always be no if you don't ask!**

6. **Talk to your physician.** In addition to taking on household chores, shopping, transportation, and personal care, 37 percent of caregivers also administer medications, injections, and medical treatment to the person for whom they care. Some 77 percent of those caregivers report the need to ask for advice about medications and medical treatments. The person they usually turn to is their physician.

    While caregivers will discuss their loved one's care with the physician, caregivers seldom discuss their own health, which is equally important. Building a partnership with a physician that addresses the health needs of the care recipient and caregiver is crucial. The responsibility of the partnership is ideally shared between you (the caregiver), the physician, and other healthcare staff. However, it will often fall to you to be assertive. Use good communication skills to ensure that everyone's needs are met—including your own. Here are some tips to help you communicate your needs better to your physician:

    a. **Prepare questions ahead of time.** Make a list of your most important concerns and problems.

Issues you might want to discuss with the physician are changes in symptoms, medications, or general health of the care recipient, your own comfort in your caregiving situation, or specific help you need to provide care.

b. **Enlist the help of the nurse.** Many caregiving questions relate more to nursing than medicine. In particular, the nurse can answer questions about various tests and examinations, preparing for surgical procedures, providing personal care, and managing medications at home.

c. **Make sure your appointment meets your needs.** For example, the first appointment in the morning or after lunch are the best times to reduce your waiting time or accommodate numerous questions. When you schedule your appointment, be sure you clearly convey the reasons for your visit so that enough time is allowed.

d. **Call ahead.** Before the appointment, check to see if the doctor is on schedule. Remind the receptionist of special needs when you arrive at the office.

e. **Take someone with you.** A companion can ask questions you feel uncomfortable asking and can help you remember what the physician and nurse said.

Enlist the medical care team as partners in care. Present what you need, what your concerns are, and how the doctor and/or nurse can help. Use specific, clear "I" statements like the following: "I need to know more about the diagnosis. I will feel better prepared for the future if I know what's in store for me" or "I am feeling rundown. I need a way for my mother to sleep at night, as I am now exhausted from being up every two hours at night with her." Be specific with your needs!

7. **Exercise.** You may be reluctant to start exercising, even though you have heard it is one of the healthiest things you can do. Perhaps you think that physical exercise might harm you or that it is only for people who are young and able to do things like jogging. Fortunately, research suggests that you can maintain or at least partly restore endurance, balance, strength, and flexibility through daily physical activities like walking and gardening. Even household chores can improve your health. The key is to increase your physical activity by exercising and using your own muscle power.

   Exercise promotes better sleep, reduces tension and depression, and increases energy and alertness. If finding time to exercise is a problem, incorporate it into your daily activities. Perhaps the care recipient can walk or do stretching exercises with you. If necessary, do frequent short exercises instead of those that require large blocks of time. Find activities you enjoy!

Walking—one of the best and easiest exercises—is a great way to get started. Besides its physical benefits, walking helps to reduce psychological tension. Walking 20 minutes a day, three times a week is very beneficial. If you can't get away for that long, try to walk for as long as you can on however many days you can. Work walking into your life. Walk around the mall, to the store, or in a nearby park. Walk around the block with a friend.

8. **Learn from your emotions.** It is a strength to recognize when your emotions are controlling you (instead of you controlling your emotions). Our emotions are messages to which we need to listen. They exist for a reason. However negative or painful, our feelings are useful tools for understanding what is happening. Even feelings such as guilt, anger, and resentment contain important messages. Learn from them, then take appropriate action. For example, when you cannot enjoy activities you previously enjoyed, and your emotional pain overshadows all pleasure, it may be time to seek treatment for depression.

Caregiving often involves a range of emotions. Some feelings are more comfortable than others. When you find that your emotions are intense, they might mean the following:

    a. You need to make a change in your caregiving situation.
    b. You are grieving a loss.
    c. You are experiencing increased stress.
    d. You need to be assertive and ask for what you need.
9. **Conclusion.** Remember: It is not selfish to focus on your own needs and desires when you are a caregiver; it's an important part of the job. You are responsible for your own self-care. Focus on the following self-care practices:
    a. Learn and use stress-reduction techniques (i.e., meditation, prayer, yoga, Tai Chi).
    b. Tend to your own healthcare needs.
    c. Get proper rest and nutrition.
    d. Exercise regularly, even if only for 10 minutes at a time.
    e. Take time off without feeling guilty.
    f. Participate in pleasant, nurturing activities, such as reading a good book or taking a warm bath.
    g. Seek and accept the support of others.
    h. Seek supportive counseling when you need it, or talk to a trusted counselor, friend, or pastor.
    i. Identify and acknowledge your feelings. You have a right to ALL of them.
    j. Change the negative ways you view situations.
    k. Set goals and take small steps to achieve them.

When it's all said and done, if you don't take care of yourself, you will not be able to take care of anyone else. Worse yet, someone may end up having to take care of you!

Resources

"Using all of your resources wisely is key for growth, which opens up success…"
~ Lincoln Patz ~

There is a multitude of resources available to help you care for your loved ones. The problem is that you probably don't have the time to research. I have put together a listing of some resources that might be helpful to you.

1. **Medical Resources**
   a. **www.samsha.gov** – SAMSHA has several products for serving older adults with mental and substance use disorders that can be useful to clinicians, service providers, and caregivers.

   Top 8 Government Programs for Seniors and Caregivers
   - Medicare
   - Supplemental Security Income (SSI)
   - The Administration on Aging (AoA)
   - Department of Veterans Affairs (VA)
   - The Americans with Disabilities Act National Network
   - The National Institutes of Health (NIH)
   - Medicaid

- State Long-Term Care Ombudsman Programs
b. **HHS.gov** – The mission of the U.S. Department of Health and Human Services (HHS) is to enhance the health and well-being of all Americans by providing effective health and human services and by fostering sound, sustained underlying medicine, public health, and social services.
c. **Eldercaredirectory.org** – This organization is committed to helping senior citizens and their caregivers find the most appropriate services and providers for their special needs, find answers to their most pressing concerns, and take advantage of government assistance programs and benefits for the elderly.
d. **Veterans Administration** (benefits.va.gov)
    i. **Elderly Veterans.** According to a recent American Community survey, the veteran population ages 65 or older numbered in excess of 18.2 million. Those veterans served in conflicts around the world, including World War II, the Korean War, the Vietnam War, and even in the Persian Gulf War. As veterans age, the Department of Veterans Affairs (VA) will provide

benefits and services that address a variety of issues, including the changing health risks they face, as well as financial challenges through VA benefits and health services.

ii. **VA Benefits.** Elderly veterans may be eligible for a wide variety of benefits available to all U.S. military veterans. VA benefits include disability compensation, pension, education and training, healthcare, home loans, insurance, Veteran Readiness and Employment, and burial.

iii. **VA Benefits for Elderly Veterans.** Two VA programs provide certain elderly veterans with an additional monetary amount if they are eligible for or receiving a VA pension benefit:

   1. **Aid and Attendance (A&A)** is an increased monthly pension amount paid if the veteran meets one of the conditions below:
      a. You require help performing daily functions, which may include bathing, eating, or dressing.

b. You are bedridden.
   c. You are a patient in a nursing home.
   d. Your eyesight is limited to a corrected 5/200 visual acuity or less in both eyes, or concentric contraction of the visual field to 5 degrees or less.
   2. **Housebound** is an increased monthly pension amount paid if you are substantially confined to your immediate premises because of a permanent disability.
e. **Healthcare for Elderly Veterans.** Geriatrics is healthcare for elderly veterans with complex needs. Extended care—also known as long-term care—is a program for veterans of all ages who need the daily support and assistance of another individual. Elderly veterans can receive geriatric and long-term care programs at home, VA medical centers, or in the community.
   i. Geriatrics Program
   ii. Long-Term Care
   iii. Eligibility for Long-Term Care
   iv. Home-Based and Community Services

  v. Nursing Home and Residential Care
  vi. Geriatrics Research

  Deciding where to spend the golden years is one of the most important decisions anyone will make. It's important to know that each state classifies assisted living and nursing homes differently and has different rules and regulations to follow to ensure senior health. The Federal and State Nursing Home & Assisted Living Regulations provides detailed information for all 50 states. Topics include how each state defines assisted living, admission and retention policies, and square feet requirements.

  f. **How to Apply.** The specific VA benefit or program web page will provide tailored information about how to apply for a particular benefit or program. Generally, servicemembers, veterans, and families can apply for VA benefits using one of the methods below:

    i. Apply online using VA.gov, **OR**
    ii. Work with an accredited representative or agent, **OR**
    iii. Go to a VA regional office and have a VA employee assist you. You can find your regional office on the VA.gov facility locator page. **OR**
    iv. File your claim using an Application for Disability Compensation and Related

Compensation Benefits (VA Form 21-526EZ). Print the form, fill it out, and send it to:

Department of Veterans Affairs
Claims Intake Center
P.O. Box 4444
Janesville, WI 53547-4444

2. **Financial Resources.** There may be shortages elsewhere, but one thing America has in abundance is seniors in debt. A recent survey indicates that 4 in 10 people over the age of 55 fear high medical bills. One in four worries they'll never pay off their debt, and 22% are afraid they won't be able to afford rent or mortgage. Below is a list of resources and charities that might help you when you need emergency financial assistance.

   a. **Organizations that help seniors**
      i. **Volunteers of America** provides help for senior citizens through a series of service programs. They offer senior benefits such as meal programs, transportation, Medicare enrollment support, nursing care, affordable housing, and more for low-income seniors.
      ii. **Senior Living** is one of the most complete databases of senior living

options, including everything from independent living to hospice-based care.

iii. **Feeding America** helps feed the hungry in the U.S. They provided nearly 166 million meals for seniors as stated in their 2020 Annual Report. This nonprofit organization works with a nationwide network of food banks to distribute meals to those in need.

iv. **Retirement Jobs** helps seniors beat age bias by matching them with companies looking for skills and expertise. They also offer resume critiques to help you land the job you want.

v. **Dental Lifeline Network** is a nonprofit organization dedicated to providing benefits programs such as access to dental care. They offer assistance for dental costs through their state or nationwide dental programs. Most of their programs operate through a network of volunteer dentists and dental labs across the U.S.

vi. **Crowdfunding to provide financial assistance for the elderly.** When you need financial help fast, crowdfunding may be your answer. With GoFundMe, there are no long waiting periods to receive your funds. If you need help with GoFundMe, search Google for "Help with GoFundMe" to find answers to top crowdfunding questions.

b. **Government financial help for seniors.** Retirement should be a peaceful time spent away from the stresses of working life. Unfortunately, many in retirement worry about how to get help with bills—both for everyday necessities and unexpected emergencies. Thankfully, the government programs listed below provide much-needed financial help for seniors.

   i. **iCanConnect.** Located in all 50 states, iCanConnect provides training and equipment for senior citizens with significant hearing and vision loss. The program helps cover the cost of computers, braille displays, smartphones, tablets, and more.

   ii. **USDA Housing Repair Grants.** Government benefits programs for seniors offered by the USDA come in the form of single-family housing repair loans and grants. These grants come with eligibility requirements, and loans are offered at a 1% fixed interest rate over a 20-year term.

iii. **Housing and Urban Development (HUD) Programs.** The U.S. Department of Housing and Urban Development offers several programs for low-income seniors who need help supplementing their income. Homeowners ages 62 and up who have paid off their mortgage may qualify for HUD's reverse mortgage program, or a subsidized property if they rent.

iv. **Low-Income Home Energy Assistance Program (LIHEAP).** This program provides federally funded assistance for families and offers help for seniors with low income who need assistance with managing the cost of home energy bills.

v. **Medicaid.** Medicaid offers all-inclusive healthcare programs for the elderly, ranging from nursing home care to medical care and prescription drugs. They also provide home- and community-based attendant care services that would otherwise be too costly to pay out of pocket.

vi. **Medicare.** Medicare beneficiaries with limited income may be eligible to participate in the Extra Help program, which provides prescription help that is worth up to $5,000 per year. The state also offers financial assistance for seniors through the Medicare Savings Programs, which can help pay Medicare premiums and deductibles.

vii. **Senior Farmers' Market Nutrition Program.** This program ensures that low-income individuals have access to locally grown produce. Eligibility restrictions apply, and the total household income must be within 185% of the federal poverty level.

viii. **Commodity Supplemental Food Program.** Individuals aged 60 and up may be eligible to receive food packages from this program.

ix. **Social Security** beneficiaries can apply for personal or spousal retirement benefits, provided they are at least 62 years old.

x. **Benefits Checkup.** The National Council of Aging's program called Benefits

Checkup is a directory of government programs that are available nationwide. There are more than 2,500 benefits programs offering help to senior citizens, from medications and healthcare to tax relief and senior employment.

   xi. **IRS Elderly Tax Credit** may help reduce the amount of tax owed each year if certain eligibility criteria are met.

c. **Help for Seniors Living Alone.** Many seniors want to continue living independently in their own homes but may need assistance with everyday activities like cooking and shopping. Thankfully, there are many programs that help seniors who are living by themselves.

   i. **Meals on Wheels** operates throughout the nation, serving home-cooked, nutritious meals to adults aged 60 and above. People with limited mobility are served at their homes, while those mobile enough are encouraged to join others for meals in a group setting.

   ii. **AmeriCorps Seniors** are volunteer workers who are seniors themselves. They help with a variety of programs, such as offering assistance with daily tasks and providing much-needed companionship to seniors.

   iii. **National PACE Association.** The Programs of All-Inclusive Care for the Elderly (PACE) offers medical, rehabilitation, personal, and other types of care so that your loved one can continue to live at home.

   iv. **ADA Paratransit** offers complementary services to eligible seniors, with no limit on the number of trips requested.

   v. **National Adult Day Services Association (NADSA)** has centers nationwide that offer numerous services to individuals who want to remain living within the community. These health and social services provide supervised care outside of the home in the daytime to seniors. Additionally, these adult day centers can also be a more cost-effective solution.

3. **Emotional Support Resources for Seniors.** As we age, mental health becomes increasingly important, especially since older adults may find themselves alone or in new living arrangements. Increased isolation brought on by COVID-19 and stay-at-home orders have

further impacted conditions that may affect elderly mental health. According to the World Health Organization (WHO), more than 20% of adults over 60 have some type of mental or neurological disorder. There are dozens of resources for seniors available through online or mobile app portals. Here are some select resources and mental health programs for older adults.

   a. **General Mental and Behavioral Health Resources**
       i. **Administration on Aging** is an agency of the U.S. Department of Health and Human Services. Its webpage offers links to resources, programs, and agencies covering a range of topics on substance abuse and mental health in the elderly.
      ii. **Behavioral Health Treatment Services Locator.** This service from the Substance Abuse and Mental Health Services Administration can help you find a nearby treatment facility for mental health aging issues.
     iii. **Health in Aging** is a service from the American Geriatrics Society that provides information for older adults and family members about mental health concerns.

iv. **MentalHealth.gov.** This site from the U.S. Department of Health & Human Services provides one-stop access to information on mental health and mental health problems.
v. **National Council on Aging** is an organization that offers a range of services and links to services for senior adults.
vi. **National Mental Health Consumers Self-Help Clearinghouse.** This directory provides comprehensive information on national and local programs providing mental health services for older adults.
vii. **Older Adults and Mental Health.** Learn about senior mental health and depression in older adults with this resource from the National Institute of Mental Health.

b. **Alzheimer's, Cognitive Impairment, and Dementia**
   i. **Alzheimer's and Related Symptoms.** This resource from the National Institute on Aging offers articles and advice for dealing with cognitive impairment and Alzheimer's.

ii. **Alzheimers.gov** is a government-run resource with links to authoritative, current information from agencies and organizations with expertise in Alzheimer's disease and dementia.
iii. **Cognitive Aging Efforts.** From the American Psychological Association, this site offers up-to-date publications, webinars, and activities related to APA cognitive aging efforts.

c. **Anxiety and Stress**
   i. **Anxiety and Older Adults: Overcoming Fear and Worry.** This article, which can be found on the Geriatric Mental Health Foundation website, discusses anxiety and its treatment.
   ii. **Anxiety in Older Adults.** This article, from Mental Health America, discusses various anxiety disorders, such as panic disorder and obsessive-compulsive disorder, and their treatments.
   iii. **Coping with Stress and Anxiety.** Learn more about how stress affects your health and what to do about it, from the American Psychological Association.

d. **Counseling Contacts**
   i. **Crisis Text Line.** Send a text from your phone to connect instantly with a crisis counselor. Text HOME to 741741.
   ii. **Disaster Distress Helpline.** Access a Substance Abuse and Mental Health Services Administration counselor ready to talk to people in emotional distress related to any natural or human-caused disaster. Call 1-800-985-5990 or text TalkWithUs to 66746.
   iii. **Suicide Prevention Hotline.** Connect with a confidential 24-hour suicide prevention hotline available to anyone in a suicidal crisis or emotional distress. Call 1-800-273-TALK (8255).
   iv. **Treatment Referral Routing Service.** This helpline offers treatment referral and information services for individuals and families facing mental and/or substance use disorders. Call 1-800-662-HELP (4357).
   v. **Veterans Crisis Line.** This service lets veterans in crisis and their families connect confidentially with qualified Department of Veterans Affairs

responders. Text 838255 or call 1-800-273-8255 and press "1" or visit their website for online chat.

4. **Caregiver Support Resources.** If you provide regular assistance, you are a caregiver. Your loved one may only need support occasionally, or your loved one may need constant care. The kind of support needed varies for each person and may also change over time. In addition to the following resources, remember spouses, brothers and sisters, children, and other relatives can also do a lot to ease your caregiving burden. Don't be afraid to reach out to them for help.

   a. **Programs**

      i. **National Family Caregiver Support Program**
         www.acl.gov/programs/support-caregivers/national-family-caregiver-support-program
         This program (NFCSP), established in 2000, provides grants to states and territories, based on their share of the population aged 70 and over, to fund a range of supports that assist family and informal caregivers to care for their loved ones at home for as long as possible.

ii. **Eldercare Locator**

www.eldercare.acl.gov

Are you a family caregiver in need of information or assistance? Are you interested in learning more about the programs and services that may be of assistance to you or your loved one? The Eldercare Locator, a public service of the U.S. Administration on Aging, is the first step to finding resources for older adults in any U.S. community. Just one phone call or website visit provides an instant connection to resources that enable older people to live independently in their communities. The service links those who need assistance with state and local area agencies on aging and community-based organizations that serve older adults and their caregivers.

iii. **Family Caregiver Alliance**

www.caregiver.org

Established in 2001, this organization works to advance the development of high-quality, cost-effective policies and programs for caregivers in every state in the country. Uniting research with public policy and services, they serve as a central source of information on caregiving and long-term care issues for policymakers, service providers, media, funders, and family caregivers throughout the country.

iv. **Caregiver Action Network (CAN)**
www.caregiveraction.org

Resources include a Peer Forum, Story Sharing platform, the Family Caregiver Toolbox, and more. CAN also provides support for rare disease caregivers at www.rarecaregivers.org.

v. **U.S. Food and Drug Administration, Office of Women's Health**
www.fda.gov/womeninclinicaltrials

Tips for Caregivers. This organization understands that caring for someone can be rewarding but challenging. Their website provides tools to help caregivers manage the care of their loved ones, as well as tips for caregivers of older adults, young children, teens, and people with special needs. The website also highlights seven tips for all caregivers to know and provides information on women and clinical trials.

vi. **Next Step in Care**

www.nextstepincare.org

Next Step in Care provides easy-to-use guides to help family caregivers and healthcare providers work closely together to plan and implement safe and smooth transitions for chronically or seriously ill patients.

vii. **WISER (Women's Institute for a Secure Retirement)**

www.wiserwomen.org

The article "Financial Steps for Caregivers: What You Need to Know About Money and Retirement" is designed to help you identify financial decisions you may face as a caregiver. The decision to become a caregiver can affect both your short-term and long-term financial security, including your own retirement. Visit the website for more information on planning for a secure retirement.

In Conclusion…

People often say, "I promised I would never put her in a nursing home," or "Dad told me he never wanted to live in one of those places."

For a variety of reasons, caregivers may choose to care for their older adult at home. As long as the situation is safe for everyone involved, keeping aging parents at home is a wonderful thing to do. However, it's important to remember that senior care is one of the toughest and most stressful jobs you'll ever have. That is why caregivers are at such high risk for burnout and serious health conditions.

So, if you're caring for your older adult at home, it's essential to pace yourself. That means you can't be running at 110% every day. You're human, and that's simply not sustainable in the long run. Pacing yourself and getting assistance help you stay as healthy as possible so you can continue providing great care.

REMEMBER:
1. Understand how much care is needed. An easy way to capture this information is to set out a notepad and write down every time you or someone else helps your older adult with something.
2. Be realistic about how much care you can provide without harming yourself. Keep in mind that if you take on too much, you will eventually burn out or develop

health issues—leaving you unable to even take care of yourself.

3. Get help with caregiving. Even though it may seem like finding caregiving help takes too much time and effort, remember that it's an investment that will pay off in the future.

4. Share caregiving responsibilities. You might be doing such an amazing job that nobody thinks you need any help caring for your older adult. So, even if you feel like you shouldn't have to say it, ask siblings or close relatives if they will take on their share of responsibility so that you can take much-needed breaks.

5. Reduce financial pressure. Caring for an older adult can also place a significant financial burden on your family. Reducing caregiving costs as much as possible helps decrease the amount of financial pressure and stress.

Just as it "takes a village to raise a child," so it is with caring for your elderly loved ones. Blessings to all who need care and those individuals who are caregivers!

About the Author

Linda H. Williams is an International Bestselling Author, Mentor, Workshop Facilitator, and Business Owner. As the Founder of "Beginning Today," Linda's organization provides support to many women's causes. Specifically, her organization works with incarcerated and formerly incarcerated women by providing life skills through the CBT platform.

Linda is a Certified Anger Management Specialist and a practitioner of Cognitive Behavior Therapy. She has written several books, including "Your Past Has Passed," "There Is Life After," "50 PLUS & Fabulous: How to Live Your Best Life," and a collection of "Inspiration Thoughts…A Journal Book Not Just for Girlfriends."

Linda has a wealth of skills and experience, with her passion being to help women live their best lives and become all that they were created to be.